FLORENCE

G000075133

Dear Visitor!

The product of one of the richest periods in European history, the Renaissance, Florence is crammed with magnificent art and architecture.

But the sheer number of 'must-see' museums, art galleries, churches and palazzos can easily overwhelm first-time visitors. With this in mind, the team behind the renowned Insight Guide series has created this Insight Pocket Guide. In these pages Insight Guides' expert on Florence, Christopher Catling, has devised a series of itineraries to help visitors establish their priorities in this beautiful city. Three full-day tours link the essential sights, such as the Duomo, the Uffizi art gallery, the Ponte Vecchio and the Pitti Palace. These are followed by a series of optional itineraries exploring other fine museums, churches and palazzos (with dips into lively markets and lovely gardens), including a walk to Fiesole and a day-trip to Pisa. All the itineraries include detailed directions on getting around and stops for rest and refreshment.

 Christopher Catling first went to Florence as an archaeologist, at a time when his taste in art was aggressively pro-modern and he did not believe anything painted before Van Gogh could hold any interest for him, especially not religious art. But Florence taught him how wrong he could be, for he soon developed a passion for Renaissance art. One of his aims in *Insight Pocket Guide: Florence* has been to provide a painless introduction to the city's wealth of art and architecture, in the hope of persuading others to take the same journey as him – 'from relative ignorance to relative enlightenment'.

Hans Höfer
Publisher, Insight Guides

Pages 2/3:
Ponte Santa
Trinita

Shopping, Dining & Nightlife

*Pages 8/9:
Detail of
Botticelli's 'Birth
of Venus'*

Calendar of Events

Practical Information

Maps

HISTORY & CULTURE

The year AD1401 marks a watershed in the history of Florence and of Western civilisation. In that year the powerful wool merchants' guild, the *Arte di Calimala*, announced that it would sponsor an artist to make new bronze doors, ornamented with Old Testament scenes, for the city's Baptistry. The aim was to outrival the splendid doors of Pisa's renowned cathedral. This was a highly prestigious project and five leading artists of the day took part in a competition to decide who should design the doors; each was asked to make a bronze relief illustrating the story of Abraham and Isaac.

In the end the judges shortlisted the candidates to two – Lorenzo Ghiberti and Filippo Brunelleschi. Their panels are now displayed in the Bargello Museum (see *Option 1, page 46*) and scholars continue to argue, even to this day, over their respective merits. The Florentine merchants decided to honour Ghiberti with the prize, but modern critics tend to prefer Brunelleschi's much more dramatic treatment of the story.

15th-century woodcut of Florentine bankers

Everyone agrees, however, that both artists produced work of revolutionary importance; their bronze reliefs not only demonstrate a new concern for realism, they also convey the full emotive force of this tragic story, in which Abraham is called upon to sacrifice his own son. The two panels mark a decisive shift in the history of artistic expression, rejecting the iconographic formalism of medieval art and looking back to classical Greek and Roman art for inspiration – in other words, the Renaissance, or 'rebirth', was under way.

Milestones of the Renaissance

Of course, Ghiberti and Brunelleschi did not invent this new style of art; rather they reflected the prevailing mood of the age. Florence was, despite constant infighting between rival families and with neighbouring cities, a proud, powerful and wealthy city. Florentine prosperity was built on the activities of the city's wool merchants, who traded in raw materials and high-quality cloth throughout Europe. These merchants saw banking as a natural extension of their activities – they invented credit banking and the city's florin became the first common European currency, widely accepted and circulated because of the purity of its gold content.

Brunelleschi's panel for the Baptistry doors

Dante, who was born in Florence in 1265 and exiled on false charges of corruption in 1302, derided the city as a 'glut of self-made men and quick-got gain'. The Florentines' nascent capitalism may have been distasteful to Dante, but it also fuelled the city's total transformation during the 15th and 16th centuries. Dante's city, whose skyline bristled with defensive towers, like New York in stone, was torn down in favour of new, classically-inspired *palazzi* (palaces). Civic pride was expressed in new churches, libraries, monasteries, hospitals and orphanages, some paid for by guilds or private patrons, others by public taxation.

All this guaranteed a stream of commissions for the artists of the day, many of whom were highly versatile, combining the skills of architect, engineer, painter, sculptor and bronze-caster. Above all, they shared a desire to create art that was appropriate to the self-confident spirit of the age, and in rejecting the stylised religious art of the preceding era they looked to nature and to the world of antiquity for their models and their subject matter.

Within this heady climate, innovations came thick and fast.

Masaccio fresco from the 'Life of St Peter'

Brunelleschi, despite losing the Baptistry doors competition, proved his superiority to Ghiberti by building the vast, gravity-defying dome that crowns the cathedral. He solved the problem of how to construct what was then the world's biggest dome by studying the ancient Roman Pantheon, and his structure, soaring above a sea of terracotta roof tiles, has come to symbolise the city.

New depths of realism were achieved by Donatello, whose statue of *St George* made for the guild of armourers in 1416 (now in the Bargello Museum – see *Option 1, page 46*) is a superb portrait of human courage tempered by anxiety. Even more startling is his bronze figure of *David*, completed in 1440 (also in the Bargello), the first realistic nude in art since antiquity and one that paved the way for Michelangelo's renowned version of the same subject.

Masaccio blazed a new trail in the technique of perspective in 1425 with his frescos on the *Life of St Peter*, in Santa Maria del Carmine (see *Day 3, page 44*) and his precise geometry was rapidly adopted by other artists. Technical innovations underlay many artistic achievements; Luca della Robbia perfected the art of glazed terracotta (see his roundels in the Innocenti orphanage – *Option 2, see page 49*) and kept the technique a secret, known only to his family, who thereby enriched themselves mightily.

Countless other artists developed new paint pigments, which accounts for the astonishing range and brilliance of the colours in the frescos and paintings of artists as diverse as Botticelli (the Uffizi – *Day 1, page 29*), Gozzoli (the Medici-Riccardi Palace – *Day 2, page 33*), and Pontormo (Santa Felicità church – *Day 3, page 39*). Above all, the towering genius of Michelangelo is evident in his huge sculptures, heroic and elemental in scale and subject matter, which have rarely been matched by any artist since.

The Medici

The Medici family ruled Florence almost continuously from 1434 until 1737. Their coat of arms is to be seen all over Florence and Tuscany; it consists of six red discs on a field of gold beneath a ducal coronet. Some say the discs represent medicinal pills and that the name, Medici, suggests descent from apothecaries. Others say the discs represent money and are a symbol of the bank founded by Giovanni di Bicci de'Medici (1360–1429) at the beginning of the 15th century. The bank expanded rapidly and was entrusted with the collection of papal revenues, thus laying the foundation of the family fortune.

The first of the family to become actively involved in political life was Giovanni's son, Cosimo de'Medici. Though he preferred not to expose himself to the full glare of public scrutiny, and never sought public office, he proved a very able behind-the-scenes manipulator. Cosimo, and subsequently his grandson, Lorenzo (dubbed Lorenzo the Magnificent), used their diplomatic skills to bring an end to the costly and inconclusive wars with rival cities that had brought Florence to the verge of bankruptcy. Both thereby helped to create the relatively prosperous and peaceful environment that enabled the city to give birth, simultaneously, to the Renaissance and to humanism.

The humanists were an informal group of like-minded men who shared a common interest in classical philosophy and ideas – one of their number, Aeneas Sylvius Piccolomini, later became Pope

Cosimo de' Medici

Pius II, even though it could be argued that the humanistic emphasis on reason, knowledge and the centrality of man in the scheme of things was incompatible with much of the current Christian dogma.

Cosimo was both a leading member of the humanist circle and its patron – paying for scholars to come to Florence to teach ancient Latin and Greek, and funding the travels of Poggio Bracciolini who specialised in tracking down lost manuscripts, including the works of Cicero, Lucretius and Quintilian. By this means he amassed a huge collection of precious works that were copied, translated and keenly discussed. Some were housed in the public library attached to the monastery of San Marco, others in the Laurentian Library (for both see *Day 2, page 31–8*). Classical ideas rapidly fed through to the artistic community who, already inspired by antique art and architecture, now found that their clients were demanding pictures of mythological, historical and secular subjects – no longer was art exclusively concerned with religious themes, and it greatly benefited from this liberalisation.

Cosimo died in 1464 leaving Florence prosperous, peaceful and with just claim to the title 'the New Rome'. His son, the sickly Piero, inherited his father's gout but did not long survive. In 1469, Lorenzo was called upon to fill his grandfather's shoes.

Lorenzo de'Medici, soaked in the humanist ideals of his grandfather, proved a worthy successor. He was renowned as a poet and he promoted the study of Dante, Boccaccio and Petrarch in the schools of Florence, thus ensuring that the Tuscan or Florentine dialect, in which these poets wrote, would become the standard for written and spoken Italian from then until the present day. Until then it had been unthinkable to read or write in anything other than Latin.

Lorenzo was equally talented as a statesman. He did much to heal ancient enmities among the rival city states of northern Italy, encouraging the most powerful to form a defensive alliance against the territorial ambitions of Charles VIII of France. Thus, when the much respected Lorenzo died in 1492, Pope Innocent VIII declared, with foresight, 'The peace of Italy is at an end.'

Florence, moreover, was left leaderless; Lorenzo's son,

Medici coat of arms

Piero de'Medici, succeeded but when, two years later in 1494, Charles VIII invaded Italy and marched on Florence, Piero simply surrendered the city and then fled. Savonarola, a firebrand preacher, stepped into the vacuum, and succeeded in convincing his fellow Florentines that the city was being punished by God for its preoccupation with profane art and pagan philosophies. He framed a republican constitution, founded on strict religious principles, and presided over a brief reign of terror during which petty misdemeanours were punished by torture; the streets blazed with 'bonfires of vanities' on which mirrors, books, paintings, musical instruments and fine clothing – all regarded as ungodly – were burned to ashes.

Soon Florence was to witness the sight of Savonarola's own body being consumed by fire. Condemned by the Pope as a heretic and excommunicated, he was arrested, tortured until he pleaded guilty to heresy, and hanged in 1498 – a fire was then lit round the scaffold in Piazza della Signoria.

The republic continued briefly under the leadership of Piero Soderini and his chancellor, Niccolo Machiavelli, but the Medici were determined to regain control of the city – not a difficult task given that Lorenzo de'Medici's second son was crowned as Pope Leo X in 1513. Leo X entered the city in triumph in 1515 and Machiavelli, after a period of imprisonment, retired to write *The Prince*, his reflections on the dirty world of *realpolitik*. Florence made one final attempt to regain its independence in 1530. Michelangelo was put in charge of the city's defences, manning the barricades around the church of San Miniato, high above the city of Florence, in a doomed attempt to keep the combined forces of the Medici, the Pope and the Holy Roman Emperor out of the city. Having supervised temporary fortifications and the hasty construction of an artillery platform round the tower of the church, Michelangelo then fled – behaviour that was later forgiven and attributed to his 'artistic temperament'.

After stout resistance, the city fell to the Medici and Alessandro de'Medici was crowned Duke of Florence, the first in a series of Medici dukes that proved corupt, debauched and tyrannical. He was murdered by his own cousin, Lorenzaccio, and was succeeded by Cosimo I, a ruthless ruler who first set about destroying all his opponents in Florence, then systematically conquering rival cities, such as Siena, to carve out the Grand Duchy of Tuscany. His 'achievements' were recorded by Vasari, whose vainglorious frescos can be seen in the Palazzo Vecchio (*Day 1, page 27*). Vasari also built the Uffizi for him (also *Day 1, page 29*). But to his credit, Cosimo I's aggressive leadership forced Tuscany into political unity and brought a new stability to the region – which then played a relatively slight

Savonarola, the firebrand preacher who regarded art as profane

19th-century Florence

role in European history.

It was not to be long before the great artists of the age deserted the city, in what Mary McCarthy, author of *The Stones of Florence*, has called 'the great diaspora of artistic talent'. From this point on, Florence would cease to be the undisputed centre of artistic excellence, and for the great achievements of the High Renaissance we have to look to elsewhere – to Rome and Venice, for example. As if to confirm that Florence had ceased to be the pre-eminent centre of the arts, Giorgio Vasari, court painter and architect to Cosimo I, Grand Duke of Tuscany, published his *Lives of the Artists* in 1550, in effect a final summing-up of the achievements of the past.

It is ironic, then, that this second Cosimo de' Medici presided over a decline in the arts, whereas his predecessors, to whom he was distantly related via the female line, had played such an important role in their encouragement. His successors, who nominally ruled Florence for another six generations, contributed little either to the smooth running of government or to promoting the arts. Yet incredibly no one challenged their right to rule and the dynasty finally expired with the death of Anna Maria in 1743.

Grand Tourists

In the 19th century, as people began to appreciate the achievements of the 'pre-Raphaelite' artists, Florence started to become the tourist destination that it is today, renowned for its awesome heritage of 15th- and 16th-century art. It became a station on the Grand Tour of first aristocratic dilettantes and members of the literati and later of the increasingly wealthy and adventurous middle classes of the rest of Europe and America.

Today, Florence is very much a busy working town, and this creates conflicts between the needs of residents and the demands made upon the city by the millions of visitors. Political debate centres round the issue of whether or not business activities should be relocated to a new satellite town, to be built between Florence and Prato, leaving the historic centre to tourism. Many Florentines are strongly opposed to this proposal since Florence itself is an inspiration to their creativity. Neither do they want Florence to lose its vitality and become a 'museum city'.

Historical Outline

59BC Foundation of the Roman colony of *Florentia*, out of which Florence is to grow.

AD250 The martyrdom of St Minias, to whom a shrine is built on the site of San Miniato church. This is the first (extant) evidence of Christianity in Florence.

4th century Building of Santa Reparata, the city's first cathedral, whose ruins survive in the Duomo (cathedral) crypt.

1125 Florence conquers and destroys neighbouring Fiesole.

13th century Florence is embroiled in factional conflict, siding with the Guelf (pro-Pope) party against Ghibelline (pro-emperor) cities, such as Pisa and Siena.

1260 Siena defeats Florence at the battle of Montaperti but is dissuaded from destroying the city.

1302 Dante, a victim of the Guelf/Ghibelline conflict, is exiled from Florence and begins his *Divine Comedy*.

1322 The Palazzo Vecchio is completed.

1348 Black Death rages through Europe and kills three-fifths of the population of Florence over the next 50 years. Boccaccio, seeing the effects of the plague in Florence, begins writing his *Decameron*.

1384 Arezzo is captured by the Florentines.

1401 Baptistry doors competition – the start of the *rinascita* (rebirth) or Renaissance.

1406 Florence conquers Pisa and gains a sea port.

1434 Cosimo de'Medici becomes a 'godfather' figure, presiding over the rise of Florence to intellectual and artistic pre-eminence.

1469 Lorenzo de'Medici comes to power.

1494 Savonarola declares Florence a republic ruled only by God.

1498 Execution of Savonarola.

1515 Florence ruled by the Medici Pope, Leo X, then by his cousin, Clement VII.

1527 Rome attacked by imperial troops and Florence rebels against papal rule.

1530 Clement VII and Emperor Charles V sign a peace treaty and unite to hold Florence at siege.

1531 Florence falls.

1555 Cosimo I becomes Duke of Florence and conquers Siena.

1570 Cosimo I is made Grand Duke of Tuscany after subjugating the region.

1610 Galileo made court mathematician to Cosimo II.

1631 Galileo excommunicated.

1737 Last Medici Grand Duke dies without an heir. The title passes to the Austrian House of Lorraine.

1808 Annexation of Tuscany by the French empire.

1848 First Italian War of Independence.

1865 Florence becomes temporary capital of the newly united Italy, pending the defeat of Rome.

1916 Mussolini is made prime minister by Victor Emmanuel.

1944 Nazis destroy parts of central Florence. Of the old bridges, only the Ponte Vecchio survives the war.

1946 Italy becomes a republic.

1966 Florence is flooded by the River Arno, triggering a huge restoration programme. Many priceless works of art lost.

1988 Florentines vote for measures to exclude traffic and control air pollution.

1993 A Mafia-placed bomb kills five people and damages the Uffizi gallery.

Florence

400 m / 0.25 miles

Day Itineraries

Orientation

The *centro storico*, the historic centre, of Florence is very compact and can be crossed on foot in less than half an hour. Strolling through the maze of mostly medieval streets is a real pleasure. You are not likely to get lost, since certain landmarks – the dome of the cathedral and the tower of the Palazzo Vecchio – can be seen from afar, and most of the streets are oriented north-south or east-west. Via de'Calzaioli ('people who make socks and shoes') is the city's spine, a broad pedestrian street connecting the Duomo to

By carriage in the Piazza della Signoria

the Piazza della Signoria where the Palazzo Vecchio has been the City Hall since 1296. The colonnades of the Uffizi gallery begin here, forming a walkway called the Piazzale degli Uffizi stretching to the the River Arno, just below the Ponte Vecchio.

Street numbering in Florence can be confusing until you realise that there are two systems: commercial premises have red numbers and residential premises blue. In written addresses, the letter 'r' after a number stands for *rosso* (red); in other words, a commercial enterprise. In the centre of Florence there are far more commercial premises than residential, so bear in mind that Via Roma 7 (blue), for example, will be considerably further down the street than Via Roma 7r (red).

Opening Times

Unless you master the opening times of Florentine museums and monuments, you could be in for a frustrating time. Remember that the majority of museums are open only in the morning (usually 9am–2pm; 1pm on Sunday) and are closed on Monday. There is a dead hole in the middle of the day when almost everything closes and you are advised to take a leisurely lunch in a restaurant, read a good book, catch up on lost sleep or go for a picnic in the Boboli Gardens. Unlike museums, churches do reopen in the afternoon (usually 3.30 or 4pm until 6 or 7pm).

On Sunday afternoon and Monday your choice is even more restricted, since many good restaurants are also closed. Do not despair; this guide has been constructed to take opening times into account (alternatively, see the table on page 91 for sights that are open when everything else is closed). However, you may still be thwarted by closures due to restoration work in progress. Thankfully, most of the damage done by the terrorist bombing of the Uffizi in 1993 has been repaired.

Follow the signs

The Duomo and the tower of the Palazzo Vecchio

The Major Landmarks

This first day in Florence will be spent visiting the most famous monuments in the centro storico – the historic centre – including the Duomo (cathedral), the Baptistry, the Piazza della Signoria and Palazzo Vecchio, the Uffizi gallery and the Ponte Vecchio.

The Duomo

If your first day in Florence happens to be a Sunday or Monday you will be able to do only the first part of this tour, since the Palazzo Vecchio and the Uffizi gallery close at 1pm on Sunday and the Uffizi is closed on Monday. Alternative sights will be proposed at appropriate points in the itinerary.

Start in **Piazza del Duomo** (Cathedral Square). The best place for kick-starting yourself into the day with a strong black *espresso* coffee is the **Sergio** bar, Piazzo del Capitolo 1, on the south side of the square, which has seats outside offering good views of the majestic cathedral dome and Giotto's campanile. From here you can get a sense of the huge scale of the cathedral, once the largest church in Christendom, and still the fourth biggest in the world.

The Duomo (the word comes from the Latin *Domus Dei*, House of God), was ostensibly built as a place of worship but, just as importantly, it symbolises Florentine civic pride and the citizens' determination always to have the biggest and the best of everything. It took almost 150 years to build (from 1294 to 1436) and even then the flamboyant neo-Gothic facade, so out of keeping with the classic restraint of the surrounding structures, was not added until the 19th century.

The bell tower, **Campanile di Giotto**, was designed by Giotto in 1331, six years before his death, and the cathedral's soaring central dome was built by Filippo Brunelleschi, the greatest architect and engineer of his day. As a tribute to Brunelleschi, no other building in Florence has been built as tall as the dome since its completion in 1436, when the cathedral was consecrated by Pope Eugenius IV.

If you cross the square from Sergio's, you can enter the cathedral by the door almost opposite, close to Giotto's bell tower (cathedral open daily 10am–5.30pm, admission free). Inside, the steps to the left lead down to the **crypt** (open daily except Sunday,

Pinnacle of the great Brunelleschi dome

10am–5pm, 3,000 lire). Here you will find Brunelleschi's simple grave. The inscription on the tomb slab compares him to Icarus, the mythical hero who learned to fly but who plunged to his death when he flew too close to the sun, melting his wings. Brunelleschi's is the only tomb in the cathedral – burial within its walls was a singular honour granted in recognition of his genius in building the dome.

The rest of the crypt contains the ruins of **Santa Reperata**, the original church on the site.

Turn left out of the crypt and right along the north wall of the cathedral. You will pass a famous fresco of **Sir John Hawkwood** on horseback painted by Paulo Uccello in 1436. Hawkwood was an English *condottiere*, or mercenary, whose hired soldiers often fought on behalf of Florence. Other cities honoured their military heroes with equestrian statues in stone or bronze; the fact that Hawkwood was commem-

Campanile di Giotto

orated only in a fresco is often cited as an example of Florentine miserliness.

Nearby you will also see a painting of Dante outside the walls of Florence, symbolising his exile – the picture was commissioned in 1465 to commemorate the bicentenary of the poet's birth.

Now you will come to the narrow door that leads up to the **Cupola del Duomo** (open daily except Sunday, 10am–5pm). If you have the stamina, pay 5,000 lire to climb the 464 spiralling stairs to the top of the Duomo for a fabulous view of the city. Though debilitating, it is an amusing trip full of little smiles and courtesies as you pass and allow passage of your fellow climbers. Until Brunelleschi, nobody had built such a massive dome since Roman times; he visited Rome to study the 2nd-century AD Pantheon in order to reinvent the ancient technique of building upwards in decreasing circles of interlocking brick.

If you have climbed the dome, you will probably not have the energy to climb the 285 steps of the **Campanile di Giotto**, on the right as you leave the cathedral (open daily 9am–7.30pm in summer, 9am–5pm winter, 5,000 lire). Save this for another day, perhaps, and walk over to the little octagonal **Battistero** (Baptistry) to the west of the cathedral. This has limited opening hours (Monday to Saturday 1–6pm, Sunday 9am–1pm, admission free) but no matter – it is the exterior that is really important.

Florentines have always exaggerated the antiquity of the Baptistry. Evidence suggests that it was built in the 6th or 7th century using Roman masonry. In the 12th century it was taken under the wing of the Calimala, the guild of wool importers, who paid for its marble cladding of green geometric designs on a white background, an innovative design admired and imitated elsewhere in Tuscany (the

Scooters in the piazza

Duomo of Florence follows its example). Set into this 10th-century building, one of the oldest in Florence, are three sets of bronze doors. Those to the south were made in the 1330s by the Pisan artist Andrea Pisano, and illustrate the *Life of St John the Baptist*, patron saint of Florence. Already they exhibit Renaissance characteristics – dynamism in the dramatic grouping of figures, fluency and immediacy, all in contrast to the rather static spirituality of the Gothic art of the 13th and 14th centuries. Pisano was several decades ahead of his time.

The Renaissance proper is conventionally dated to 1401 when a competition was held to select an artist for the remaining doors (see *History and Culture*). The winner, Lorenzo Ghiberti (1378–1455), first made the doors that fill the north entrance, illustrating New Testament scenes, completed in 1424. He then made the superb **Paradise Door** (Porta del Paradiso) or the east entrance facing the cathedral, so called because Michelangelo hailed these doors as suitable for the entrance to paradise. What you see now are casts of the original panels, illustrating Old Testament scenes (the originals, completed in 1452, are now under restoration and will eventually be displayed in the Museo dell'Opera del Duomo – see *page 51*). The doorframes, however, are original and contain portrait busts of 24 leading Renaissance artists – Ghiberti himself is the bald-headed figure, third up from the bottom in the centre of the doors.

Renaissance man?

When you have seen enough, walk down the south flank of the cathedral, to the east end, and turn right down Via del Proconsolo. On the left you will pass No 12, the **Palazzo Nonfinito** (the Unfinished Palace) begun by Bountalenti in 1593 and never completed; it contains the **Anthropology Museum** (open Thursday, Friday, Saturday and the third Sunday in every month, 9am–1pm, admission free) containing interesting relics of Captain Cook's last voyage to the Pacific. Take the first right, Via del Corso, passing the **Banco di Toscana** (Bank of Tuscany) on the right – the exchange rate here is good and the banking hall features a fresco of the Virgin, St John and St Zenobius.

Opposite the bank, go through a tunnel into Via Santa Margherita where, on the left, is the little church built in 1200 where Dante first set eyes on Beatrice Portinare, the daughter of a wealthy banker, whom he was to idealise in his poetry. The church is often used for baroque chamber music and organ recitals – see the notice at the entrance (church open Monday to Saturday 9am–noon and 3–6.30pm, Sunday 9am–noon, admission free).

At the end of the street, on the right, is the **Casa di Dante**

(Monday to Saturday 9.30am–12.30pm and 3.30–6.30pm, Sunday 9.30am–12.30pm, closed Wednesday, 4,000 lire). This much restored medieval house with its truncated 13th-century tower is claimed as Dante's birthplace and contains a small museum on the poet's life and work – the downstairs rooms (entrance free) are often used for exhibitions of contemporary art.

Turn right in Via Dante Alighieri and head straight on, ignoring side turnings, to Via de'Calzaiuoli (passing the renowned ice-cream shop, Perche Noi, on the left at Via dei Tavolina 19r). Opposite is the church of **Orsanmichele** (daily 8am–noon and 3–6.30pm, admission free). Walk round the church, to the right, down Via dei Tavolini, to study the statues in the wall niches. Each of these niches belonged to one of the city's powerful guilds, who commissioned artists to portray their patron saints. The most famous statue, Donatello's *St George*, is now replaced by a copy; the original can be seen in in the Bargello Museum (*page 46*).

At the back, Orsanmichele is linked to the 13th-century Palazzo del'Arte della Lana (Wool Guild Palace) by an aerial corridor. The entrance to the church is below and its centrepiece is Andrea Orcagna's elaborate tabernacle (1459), decorated with scenes from the *Life of the Virgin*, enclosing Bernardo Daddi's painting of the *Madonna* (1347). Turn left out of the church, left again in Via de' Lamberti, passing Donatello's statue of *St Mark* in the first niche, then right in Via de' Calzaiuoli, to **Piazza della Signoria**.

The spacious square is now traffic-free (although smoky buses still roar along its side). Towering over everything is the battlemented facade and campanile of the **Palazzo Vecchio**, built as the seat of city government between 1299 and 1322. This dwarfs even the huge heroic figure of *David* (a copy – Michelangelo's original is in the Accademia, see *Day 2*), Bandinelli's rather lumpy figure of *Hercules* (1534) and the licentious nymphs of Ammanati's *Neptune Fountain* (1575). These works of art, all fronting the palace, symbolise Florence in various ways – for example, David as a figure of defiance against tyranny, Hercules as the mythical founder of the city and Neptune as a metaphor for the city's naval fleet created by Cosimo I. To the right, sheltering under the **Loggia dei Lanzi** (named after Cosimo I's bodyguard, the lancers) are several antique statues and Giambologna's renowned *Rape of the Sabine Women* (1583).

If you are ready for lunch the **Pizzeria Il David** is the best bargain in the square (in the evening, Il Bargello – elegant as it is –

The towering Palazzo Vecchio

A fresco in the Palazzo Vecchio

has a fixed price dinner for about $15). The classy **Rivoire** offers ice-cream and pastries (closed Monday).

Your choice will partly depend on the day of the week – as will your next move. The afternoon will be spent visiting the Palazzo Vecchio and the Uffizi but not if it is a Saturday, when the Palazzo Vecchio is closed: instead you might like to visit the Bargello (*Option 1*) or spend longer in the Uffizi. If it is a Sunday afternoon, when both are closed, you might like to walk off lunch by heading for San Miniato (*Option 5*), as Florentines do on a Sunday. If it is Monday, you can visit the Palazzo Vecchio, but not the Uffizi; instead, try the excellent Museo dell'Opera del Duomo (*Option 3*).

After lunch cross the Piazza della Signoria again, negotiating the crowds, the pigeons and the horse-drawn carriages. Passing *David*, climb the steps of the **Palazzo Vecchio** to enter the delightful *cortile* (entrance courtyard) with its charming *putto* and dolphin fountain, Vasari's copy of an original made by Verrocchio in 1470. This courtyard is gracefully feminine and its frescos, by Vasari, depict Austrian cities, which were designed to make Joanna of Austria feel at home on the occasion of her marriage to Francesco de'Medici in 1565.

Upstairs, though, the tone is aggressively masculine, as you will find as you turn right up the steps that lead to the **Quartieri Monumentali** (Monday to Friday 9am–7pm, Sunday 8am–1pm, closed Saturday, 10,000 lire). The first room that you come to is the vast

The cortile of the Palazzo Vecchio

Salone dei Cinquecento, which was used for meetings of the Florentine Grand Council under the reign of Savonarola, the religious despot who regarded artists as heretics. It was later transformed by Giorgio Vasari whose frescos depict the military victories of Duke Cosimo I. Statues of writhing, wrestling figures, by Michelangelo, Vincenzo de'Rossi and Giambologna line the walls. Just off the Salone dei Cinquecento is the little study of Francesco de'Medici, dating to 1575, a suitable retreat for the reclusive prince whose parents, Duke Cosimo I and Eleonora di Toledo, are depicted on the walls.

Beyond lies a whole suite of rooms, all frescoed by Vasari, used by the various Medici Popes and one-time rulers of Florence; several offer fine views over the city. The rooms of Eleonora di Toledo are among the most attractive, with their ceiling frescos depicting feminine virtue.

The magnificient Sala dei Gigli

After this comes the most magnificent of all the chambers, the **Sala dei Gigli**, whose walls are covered in the gold fleur-de-lis (lily) symbol of Florence. Here, too, you will find a delicate marble statue of St John the Baptist (patron saint of Florence) as a boy, and Donatello's *Judith and Holofernes* (1460), originally placed in the Piazza della Signoria after the expulsion of the Medici in 1494 – once again a biblical story (the virtuous Judith slaying the drunken tyrant Holofernes) was designed to symbolise Florentine triumph over despotism. Just off the Sala dei Gigli is the **Cancellaria**, which displays a painting and a bust of Niccolo Machiavelli who used the room as his office whilst chancellor.

Steps now lead down and out of the Palazzo Vecchio; returning through the *cortile*, exit and turn left for the entrance to the **Galleria degli Uffizi** (Tuesday to Saturday 9am–7pm, Sunday 9am–1pm, closed Monday, 12,000 lire). This complex was built by Vasari, from 1560, to house the administrative offices of Duke Cosimo I (hence its name – *uffici* simply means offices) as well as the artistic

The Ponte Vecchio, built in 1345 and occupied by jewellers' shops since 1593

masterpieces commissioned or collected by the Medici. The art collection is outstanding and includes antique statuary, displayed in the corridors, while the paintings, displayed chronologically in the side room, include some of the world's most famous early Renaissance works. The damage that was caused by a terrorist bomb in 1993 was less serious than at first thought. The star of the collection is Botticelli, whose restored allegory of spring, *Primavera* (1480), and *Birth of Venus* (1485) are displayed in Room X.

Exhaustion sets in about halfway round the gallery, but you can refresh yourself in the café (at the end of the west corridor, beyond Room XLV) which sits over the Loggia dei Lanzi with good views of the Piazza della Signoria. Save some time to see the later works in the west wing, especially those of Titian (Room XXVII) and Caravaggio (XLII).

From the Uffizi exit, turn right down to the river Arno and right again to reach the **Ponte Vecchio** (old bridge), the 'golden bridge' of Florence. Wander with the crowds, enjoying the views from the bridge and the bustle of traders, tourists and buskers.

For a guide to the best shops on the bridge see the *Shopping* section of this book (*pages 68–71*). There are also scores of good restaurants nearby – just south of the bridge, for example, you can dine elegantly *al fresco* in Piazza Santa Felicità at **Celestino** (tel: 296574) or **Di Bibo** (tel: 298554); alternatively you can eat authentic and inexpensive pizza at **Borgo Antic**, or at the **Pizzeria Dante**, Piazza Nazario Sauro (just south of the Ponte alla Carraia, tel: 293215).

Detail from Botticelli's 'Birth of Venus'

Michelangelo and the Medici

Today you will hit the Michelangelo trail, visiting some of his best works and unravelling his somewhat ambivalent relationship with the Medici family; in between you will visit the markets around San Lorenzo and some very upmarket shops in the Santa Maria Novella district.

Head as early in the day as possible for the **Galleria dell'Accademia**, Via Ricasoli 60 (Tuesday to Saturday 9am–2pm, Sunday 9am–1pm, closed Monday, 10,000 lire) because this gallery attracts a huge number of visitors and long queues rapidly build up, especially at Easter and in the peak summer months. If you find a queue has already formed, don't despair – it moves quite quickly and you should not have to wait much more than 15 minutes to get in (if you've time for a coffee first try the typical neighbourhood bar on the corner of Via Ricasoli and Via degli Alfani, just south of the Accademia entrance).

The queues can be explained in two words: Michelangelo's *David* (1504) – the original statue, as opposed to the copy that now stands in front of the Palazzo Vecchio. Its current setting is far from satisfactory – it was moved here in 1873 as a precaution

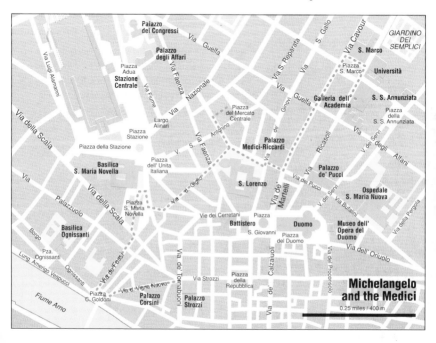

Michelangelo
and the Medici

0.25 miles / 400 m

against weathering and pigeon droppings – but the towering figure still exerts a magnetic force on visitors. *David* is both a powerful celebration of the adolescent male body (though somewhat distorted, with overlarge head and hands) and a symbol of Florentine aspiration – her citizens liked to think of themselves as brave combatants, ready to fight any tyrannical Goliath who threatened their liberty (for which read the Pope, the Medici, the Holy Roman Emperor, neighbouring city states or any other temporary enemy).

Michelangelo, who had begun his apprenticeship at 13 at the sculpture school in the Medici gardens, himself shared these republican instincts. He offered to carve *Samson overcoming a Philistine* to symbolise the new republic after Piero de'Medici fled the city in 1494. He never fulfilled his promise because he was too busy doing other things – fulfilling commissions, in fact, for those same enemies of the republic, the Medici popes. Part of the enigma of Michelangelo is the fact that he both fought against the Medici (literally in 1530, during the siege of Florence) and depended on their patronage. On display here is the unfinished *Quatri Prigioni* (*Four Slaves*), originally intended for the tomb of Pope Julius II. From 1534 until his death 30 years later Michelangelo lived in Rome. His work is the highlight of the Accademia, but there are some other interesting works – in particular, do not miss the excellent plaster models made by Lorenzo Burtolini (1797–1850) displayed in the **Salone delle Toscane**. These are preliminary working models, which were then copied in sculpted marble to produce the final work of art, and they include outstanding portrait busts and funerary monuments.

From the Accademia, turn right and head for the **Piazza San Marco**. If it is term time you will weave your way through chatting groups of art students who are studying at the Accademia, which was founded by Vasari, with Michelangelo as one of its members, in 1563. You will also pass, almost opposite the gallery exit, the Libreria LEF book-

A student at the Accademia

shop (Via Ricasoli 105); if you are interested in art and architecture you will find a comprehensive stock of books, postcards and posters here.

Straight ahead, in Piazza San Marco, you will find the **Museo di San Marco** (Tuesday to Saturday 9am–2pm, Sunday 9am–1pm, closed Monday, admission 6,000 lire) housed in a group of conventual buildings. Many famous names are connected with San Marco. Cosimo de' Medici paid for the building of this monastery, which was occupied

Detail of Michelangelo's 'David'

by Dominican friars from the nearby hill town of Fiesole in 1436. Fra Angelico spent most of his life within its walls and the museum contains most of his paintings, as well as some superb frescos: his *Crucifixion* (1442) in the Chapter House, his *Annunciation* at the top of the staircase leading to the dormitory, and a series of almost abstract pictures, designed as aids to religious contemplation, in cells 1 to 10 of the dormitory (other artists were involved in the remaining cell paintings). Savonarola was made prior of the convent in 1491 and his cells (Nos 12 to 14) contain various mementoes.

As you emerge from San Marco, look to the right-hand (northwest) corner of the square, where there is a house ornamented with rams' heads. This stands on the site of the Medici garden in which Cosimo de'Medici displayed his collection of antique sculptures and where, in the attached school of art, the young Michelangelo studied drawing.

Now head down Via Cavour to reach No 1, the **Palazzo Medici-Riccardi**, on the right. This somewhat grim (and deliberately unostentatious) palace was built for Cosimo de'Medici between 1444 and 1464. It was from here that Cosimo and his heirs operated as unofficial rulers of Florence until Piero fled the city in 1494. The building is undergoing restoration, but you can go into the courtyards, whose walls are studded with antique inscriptions. If, by the time you visit, the **Cappella dei Magi** is open again, do go in and see the stunningly colourful fresco of the *Journey of the Magi*; this was painted by Benozzo Gozzoli in 1459 and members of the Medici family are depicted amongst the royal retinue.

Leaving the palace, turn right and right again, in Via de'Gori, and you will plunge into the midst of the huge and bustling San Lorenzo street market. There will be time to explore this later on – now the aim is to see the church of San Lorenzo and the Medici tombs before they close. As you weave through the stalls you will see an equestrian statue of *Giovanni delle Bande Nera*, the warrior father of Duke Cosimo I, by Bandinelli (1540).

To the left of the statue **San Lorenzo** church is entered through a door in the rough unfinished facade (open daily 7am–noon and 3.30–5.30pm, admission free). The interior was mainly designed by Brunelleschi and is remarkable for the elegant sobriety of the grey stone and white walls. Just before the central domed crossing are two huge marble pulpits carved by Donatello with scenes from the *Passion* and *Resurrection of Christ*. To the north of the pulpits, Bronzino's huge fresco, depicting the *Martyrdom of St Lawrence* (1569), is unmissable. To the left, and often overlooked, is a more recent painting by Pietro Annigoni (1910–88) of the young Jesus with Joseph in a carpenter's workshop.

Between the two a doorway leads out to the serene cloister, with views over to Giotto's campanile, and immediately to the right a staircase leads up to the **Biblioteca Laurenziana**, or Laurentian Library (Monday to Saturday 10am–noon, closed Sunday, admission free). The library, with its extraordinary vestibule and staircase, was designed by Michelangelo from 1524. His client was the Medici Pope, Clement VII, and the library was built to house part of the famous collection of antique Greek and Latin manuscripts collected by Cosimo and Lorenzo de'Medici. Depending on what's currently on display you may see Pliny the Younger's hand-written text; a 1436 printing of Plutarch's *Moralia* (Morals) and a Greek edition (1496) of the works of the 15th-century humanist Poliziano with handwritten notations.

Return through the church, turn left at the exit doors and weave round to the rear of San Lorenzo for the last, and perhaps greatest, example of Michelangelo's work for the Medici. The entrance to the **Cappelle Medicee** (Medici Chapels) is on Piazza Madonna degli Aldobrandini (Tuesday to Saturday 9am–2pm, Sunday 9am–1pm, closed Monday, 9,000 lire).

When you enter you will first pass through the extraordinary **Cappella dei Principi** (Chapel of the Princes), whose walls are covered in costly multi-coloured marble and whose enormous sarcophagi commemorate the 16th- and 17th- century Grand Dukes of Tuscany. From here a corridor leads to the **Sagrestia Nuova** (New Sacristy) designed by Michelangelo – sober by contrast and yet containing some stupendous sculptures.

The modest tomb of Lorenzo de'Medici is marked by Michelangelo's unfinished *Madonna and Child*. To the left is the tomb of Lorenzo's grandson, also called Lorenzo (1492–1519), draped with the figures of *Dawn* and *Dusk*, while opposite is the tomb of Lorenzo's son, Giuliano, with the figures of *Night* and *Day*. These awesome figures, symbolising the temporal and the eternal forces of nature, were carved fitfully between 1520 and 1533. Ironically, whilst still working on them, Michelangelo was, at the same time, involved in the battle to keep Florence an independent republic against the besieging forces of the Medici

In the Mercato Centrale

(see *History & Culture*). When that battle was lost it is thought that Michelangelo hid from his Medici patrons in this very chapel. A small room contains charcoal sketches on the walls made by Michelangelo at this time.

From the sombre mood of the Medici Chapel, you plunge back into the mêlée of Florentine street life. If you want to eat, turn left into Via del Giglio, where there is a good choice of restaurants. **Ganesh**, at 28r, is a smart Indian restaurant serving mild curries, tandoori and vegetarian dishes (closed Monday and Tuesday) and opposite, at 49r, is the up-market **Gran Ristorante de'Medici** where you can eat a full-blown *bistecca alla fiorentina*, or a simple pizza (closed Monday). If you are on a budget, you can snack in the Central Market – in which case turn right out of the Medici Chapel, then left in Via dell'Ariento, passing through the open-air San Lorenzo market. The stalls immediately adjacent to the church are geared to tourists and sell T-shirts,

Straw hats for sale

leatherwork and souvenirs. The deeper in you go, the more stalls you will find catering to the needs of ordinary Florentines, selling bargain-priced clothes, shoes, fabrics and table linen.

In 1990 the city administration tried to close the market down – at least, that part of the market that crowds around San Lorenzo church. Eventually the police gave up on their task in the face of determined resistance from the stallholders. As you walk through the market, do not neglect the little shops either side of the street, almost hidden by the stalls, where you will find all sorts of necessities for sale.

Halfway up, on the right, is the entrance to the huge **Mercato Centrale** (Central Market). The stalls on the ground floor sell an abundance of meat, fish and cheese, while upstairs, under the towering glass and cast-iron roof, you can buy fruit, vegetables and flowers – and you will not find better quality or keener prices than here. Also upstairs is a delightful bar where you can enjoy a coffee or drink immersed in the animated buzz of conversation of shoppers and stall holders. You can also sample some Florentine specialities sold from the cooked-meat stalls or cafés downstairs – *lampredotto* (pig's intestine) or *trippa* (tripe) eaten with *panino* (bread roll) are perhaps not to everyone's taste, but *porchetta* (roast suckling pig) is delicious.

Head next along Via del Giglio to **Piazza Santa Maria Novella** and its **church** (open daily 7–11.30am and 3.30–6pm, admission free). There is plenty to see here to fill an hour or so. The vast square itself was originally used for chariot races and the church has a graceful facade of green and white marble, incorporating the name of the Rucellai family along with their symbol or trademark – a billowing ship's sail, representing trade. The wealthy family, who paid the architect Alberti to build the facade in 1470, formed a marriage alliance with the Medici – hence you will also notice that family's ring-and-ostrich-feather symbol amongst the complex geometric patterning.

Inside, on the wall of the third chapel on the left, is Masaccio's renowned fresco of the *Trinity, Mary and St John* (1427), whose architectural setting and three-dimensional qualities make it a landmark in the development of perspective in early Renaissance art. Behind the high altar see the charming and colourful frescos of Ghirlan-

Restoring old treasures

daio, illustrating the *Life of the Virgin* and of *St John the Baptist* (1485–90). These repay detailed study and give a good idea of the clothing worn by well-to-do Florentines in the late 15th century, and the luxury and comfort of their homes. Equally compelling are Filippino Lippi's frescos in the Strozzi Chapel, to the right of the altar (1497–1502).

There are more frescos of note to be seen in the cloister alongside the church, including Uccello's dramatic *Noah and the Flood* (1450), but you will probably have to return another time to see on another occasion, thanks to perverse opening times (cloister open Monday to Saturday 9am–2pm, Sunday 8am–1pm, closed Friday, 4,000 lire).

For now, head left across the square, into Piazza degli Ottaviani and Via de' Fossi. The latter boasts some interesting shops. **Saleh** (65r) sells good modern jewellery, **Neri** (57r) sells antiques and **G. Lisio** (41r) makes and sells superb handwoven textiles and tapestries. At **Antonio Frilli** (26r) you can buy reproduction sculptures of the most famous statues in Florence, in every imaginable size, plus fountains in marble, erotic groups in the style of Canova and some original art nouveau works – most, though, are priced in millions of lire.

At the bottom of the street, leading to Piazza C Goldoni, there are more good shops worth investigating: in Borgo Ognissanti, to the right, they include the **BM** English-language bookshop (4r) and **Fallani Best** (15r) which sells art nouveau and art deco pieces. Alternatively, turning left brings you to Via della Vigna Nuova and Via de' Tornabuoni, both lined with chic boutiques and couturiers (see *Shopping*).

If you manage to resist spending too much money, then reward yourself with a table for tonight in the elegant setting of the **Cantinetta Antinori**, at the top of Via de' Tornabuoni (see *Eating Out*); alternatively seek out the rather Gothic setting of **Trattoria Garga** (Via del Moro 48r, Tel: 298898, closed Monday). The décor here is definitely freakish but the atmosphere is lively and the cooking highly creative.

Oltrano: Pitti Palace and Boboli Gardens

Today's itinerary heads south to Oltrarno – literally 'beyond the Arno' – to visit the Pitti Palace, with its five museums, the Boboli Gardens for outstanding views, and the Brancacci Chapel for Masaccio's great frescos on the Life of St Peter.

Cross the river by the **Ponte Vecchio** (literally 'Old Bridge'), built in its present form in 1345 and the only one in the city that did not get blown up in August 1944 by retreating Nazis (the others have since been reconstructed). As you cross the bridge, note the corridor on the left-hand side, high above the jewellers' shops, which is known as the **Corridoio Vasariano** (Vasari's Corridor), named after its designer. It links the Palazzo Vecchio, seat of the Tuscan administration, with the Palazzo Pitti, home of the Medici Grand Dukes from 1550. The rulers of Florence and Tuscany could walk along this corridor without having to mingle with the common herd. On the opposite side of the river, as you walk down Via de' Guicciardini, you will see the corridor again in front of **Santa Felicità** church, on the left.

Have a look inside this church, which has two remarkable works by the Mannerist artist, Pontormo, an *Annunciation* and a *Deposi-*

tion (both of 1525–28). Mary Mc-Carthy (in *The Stones of Florence*) professed to find these works decadent, but she accurately described their extraordinary colours – peppermint pink, orchid, gold-apricot, pomegranate and iridescent salmon!

Just opposite the palace look for the fascinating mask store called Firenze of Papier Mâché and have a drink at the charming sidewalk bar simply called Il Caffe.

The **Palazzo Pitti** (Pitti Palace) was begun in the late 1450s for the banker Luca Pitti, but the cost of the building brought him to the verge of bankruptcy and his heirs sold it to Eleonora di Toledo, the Spanish-born wife of Duke Cosimo I, in 1549. The Medici moved here in 1550 and from then onwards it served as the home of Tuscany's rulers, gradually being expanded to its present immense bulk. It now houses three museums, and there are two more in the Boboli Gardens behind. We will spend the morning in the **Galleria Palatina**, which contains outstanding works of art (Tuesday to Saturday 9am–2pm, Sunday 9am–1pm, closed Monday, 8,000 lire). If, however, you are interested in court and theatrical costume, you should visit the excellent **Galleria del Costume** (same hours, 6,000 lire). This is located in the east wing of the palace, but can be entered only from the Boboli Gardens, so you must get your ticket at the front of the palace.

The entrance to the first-floor Galleria Palatina lies to the right of the courtyard where a flight of steps leads up to a suite of apartments with frescos by Pietro da Cortona (1641–65). They illustrate, allegorically, the stages in the education of a prince as he leaves behind the joys of adolescent love (symbolised by a pneumatic Venus) to learn the arts of science, war, and justice under the respective tutelage of Apollo, Mars and Jupiter.

Bust on the Ponte Vecchio

Apart from these rich frescos, each room contains a wealth of art. In the Sala de Venere (Venus), for example, look out for Titian's portrait of a woman known as *La Bella* (the Beautiful), painted in 1536, and Canova's statue of *Venus* emerging from her bath.

In the Sala di Apollo is another Titian, the rather more erotic than repentant *Maddalena* (Mary Magdalene). Rubens's vast canvas, the *Consequences of War* (1638), is the highlight of the Sala di Marte (Mars), a bleak allegory of the atrocities being perpetrated in Europe at the time of the Thirty Years' War. Far more serene is Raphael's *Donna Valeta* (1516), said to be a portrait of Lucrezia delle Rovere, in the Sala di Giove (Jove), and the same artist's tender *Madonna della Seggiola* (1515) in the Sala di Saturna (Saturn).

The opulence of the palace

The numerous rooms that lie beyond are remarkable for the opulence of their decorations. In particular, do not miss Napoleon's bathroom, designed in 1813 as a part of a suite of apartments for the Emperor after he had conquered northern Italy. It is decorated with stucco nymphs and four marble Nereids – who would not love such a sumptuous bathroom as this?

Even so, the weight of crimson, gold and heavy ornate furniture can become oppressive after a while, and it is a relief to escape back into the palace courtyard and head for the open green spaces of the **Giardino di Boboli**, or Boboli Gardens (daily 9am–4.30pm in November to February, 9am–5.30pm March and October, 9am–6.30pm April, May and September, 9am–7.30pm June to August, closed Monday, entrance free for over-60s and under 18s). They were laid out from 1550 onwards and are among the largest and most splendid formal gardens in Italy. The gardens can be entered either from the palace courtyard or from a gate 200 metres/yards beyond the palace on Via Romana.

In the palace courtyard is a humorous marble statue of Duke

Cosimo's court dwarf riding on a turtle. Straight ahead is a somewhat fantastical grotto whose inner walls are decorated with sheep, goats and shepherds playing among the stalactites. Rather incongruously, Michelangelo's unfinished carvings of the *Four Slaves* were placed here too by Duke Cosimo (today they have been replaced by copies – the originals are in the Accademia – see *Day 2*). Further inside you will come across *Paris seducing Helen of Troy* in Vincenzo de'Rossi's erotic marble grouping and, almost hidden from view, Giambologna's delicious *Venus* emerging from her bath.

Follow the broad path uphill, past the pool with its Neptune statue and an ancient Egyptian obelisk looted by the Romans from Heliopolis in 30BC. On the next terrace is the statue of *Abundance* beneath the walls of the Forte di Belvedere. If you turn left and follow the path beneath the fortress walls you will eventually come to a gate which may be unlocked, in which case you'll have access to **Forte di Belvedere,** built as a private fortification by Duke Ferdinando in 1590. The fort is well named for the views from its walls really are stunning; in one direction you look over the city centre whilst in the other you look over a rural landscape of olive groves and cypress trees to the church of San Miniato and up to the ancient astronomical observatory, the Torre del Gallo

Keeping to the right downhill brings you to the little baroque **Kaffeehaus** (open 10am–5.30pm) built in 1776. The interior is frescoed with garden scenes and the intimate terrace alongside, with its lovely view over Florence, is a perfect spot to reflect upon

The carefully constructed Boboli Gardens

the history of the gardens over lunch. The Kaffeehaus serves pizza, sandwiches, ice-cream and drinks.

One year after the Boboli Gardens opened in 1550, Baccio Bondinelli who had lived both in Bramante's papal garden at the Vatican and in Raphael's Villa Madama, wrote to Grand Duke Cosimo I: 'It seems to me that this field I have seen has been so well placed by nature, I have seen no other like it.' Baccio specialised in creating floral ornaments and fountains for ducal gardens. Over the years, the Medicis experimented with growing potatoes, pineapples and mulberries, continuing the tradition of botanical cultivation. The diarist John Evelyn, who visited in 1644, noted roses grafted onto orange trees and 'much topiare'.

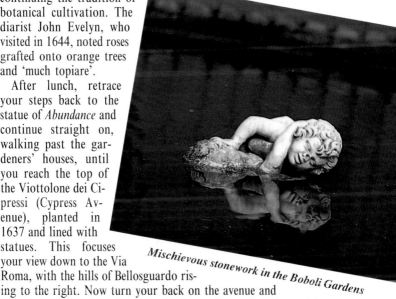

After lunch, retrace your steps back to the statue of *Abundance* and continue straight on, walking past the gardeners' houses, until you reach the top of the Viottolone dei Cipressi (Cypress Avenue), planted in 1637 and lined with statues. This focuses your view down to the Via

Mischievous stonework in the Boboli Gardens

Roma, with the hills of Bellosguardo rising to the right. Now turn your back on the avenue and take the path to the left, past a broken column, then descend by the path to the right which takes you down to the rear of the Pitti Palace again.

Here, the doorway flanked by two lions leads to the **Galleria del Costume**, the Costume Gallery, containing court and theatrical dress in the 18th and 19th centuries.

Turn left to descend a wide avenue and take the first right to exit the garden into Via Romana. Turn right and walk up this street, taking the third turning left, Via Mazzetta; you may want to browse for a while in the many good antique shops in this area, especially in Via Maggio. Via Mazzetta leads to the leafy **Piazza Santo Spirito** where, depending on the time of day, you might find a street market in full swing.

This part of the city is very different from the historic centre north of the river – bustling, lively and authentically Florentine. Walking along the right-hand side of the square, note **Caffe Ricchi** (9r) with its tables and chairs under the trees; you may want to return here for an evening drink and dinner in the **Trattoria Borgo**

Antic (6r). Next door you can watch carpenters at work producing intricate mouldings for reproduction furniture while the antique shop **Il Tempo** (1r) sells toys and 1950s memorabilia. At the head of the square is the church of **Santo Spirito** (open daily 8am–noon and 4pm–6pm, admission free). This is regarded as Brunelleschi's masterpiece, a superb example of Renaissance classicism with a serene interior, begun in 1436.

Leaving the church, walk up the right-hand side of the square. If you have fallen in love with Florence, you may want to take a look in the windows of real estate agent, R Agostini (19r) to see if any apartment takes your fancy – small flats for a mere 200 million lire. The workshop at 17r makes lovely reproduction baroque picture frames and the Antica Trattoria Oreste (16r) is another potential dinner spot.

Turn right in Via Sant'Agustino, past tempting food shops and the little bookshop at 42r which has a display of Edwardian erotic postcards in the window – plump matrons playing at being the Three Graces. Cross Via de'Serragli (the name does not refer to seraglios, or brothels, but to the Serragli family) and continue down Via Santa Monica to reach the huge **Piazza del Carmine**.

The church of Santa Maria del Carmine was destroyed by fire in 1771 and rebuilt. However, by great good fortune, the **Cappella Brancacci**, alongside to the right, was spared (Monday to Saturday 10am–5pm, Sunday 1–5pm, closed Tuesday, 5,000 lire). Once inside this tiny chapel you are brought face to face with the newly restored frescos on the *Life of St Peter* begun by Masolino, continued by Masaccio from 1425 until his death in 1428 and completed by Filippino Lippi in 1480. Masaccio's contribution has been hailed as a superb example of the emerging Renaissance style, remarkable for the clearly worked out perspective and the use of *chiaroscuro*, light and shade, to highlight the central figures. St Peter, a serene figure wearing a saffron toga and blue tunic,

Erotic postcards in Via Sant'Agustino

A social afternoon in the piazza

moves amongst the poor and the crippled, distributing alms and working miracles, against the backdrop of the streets and buildings of 15th-century Florence. So intimate is the space, and so forceful the work, that you will feel part of the crowd that witnesses these events.

Masaccio's work is mainly in the upper tier of the fresco and includes his vigorous and dramatic *Expulsion from Paradise*, in which the figures of Adam and Eve, no longer beautiful as in Masolino's *Temptation* scene opposite, are racked with misery. The scenes in the lower tier, mostly by Fil-

Piazza Santo Spirito

ippino Lippi, are equally distinguished but it is Masaccio, inevitably, who wins all the praise for his pioneering work and youthful genius (Masaccio was a mere 27 years old when he died).

Leaving the chapel, cross the square to the right, passing **Dolce Vita** (6r) – a popular night spot (see the section on *Nightlife, page 78*). As I have already noted, there are plenty of good spots in this district for enjoying an evening drink or meal. Alternatively you can simply return to the Ponte Vecchio by turning right in Borgo San Frediano and just following your nose.

Option 1. The Bargello and Santa Croce

This morning's visit is to an outstanding collection of sculpture in the Bargello Museum; you can also sample the world's best ice-cream and pay homage at the tombs of Galileo, Machiavelli and Michelangelo.

Start in the **Piazza di San Firenze**. If you take coffee in the tiny **Bar Nazionale** (No 7r) your breakfast companions are likely to be lawyers who work in the law courts of the **Tribunale**, the baroque building on the opposite side of the bustling square. This corner of Florence has always been associated with enforcement of the law; the Bargello, which you are about to visit, once served as the city prison and place of execution.

First, though, make a quick detour to the **Badia Fiorentina**, the church opposite the Bargello on the corner of Via dei Proconsolo and Via Dante Alighieri. The church of a Benedictine abbey found in 978 but considerably altered in 1627–31, it merits a visit on account of a delightful painting by Filippino Lippi, the *Apparition of the Virgin to St Bernard* (1485) just inside the door. The Virgin is depicted as a full-blooded woman and the children that surround her are the children of the Florentine streets. The church's other attraction lies through a door immediately to the right of the high altar; if it is open, walk up the stairs to the peaceful **Chiostro degli Aranci** (named after the orange trees

Bronze bird at the Bargello

that, sadly, no longer grow here). The lovely cloister, adorned with damaged 15th-century frescos depicting the miracles of St Bernard by Rossellino, offers fine views of the Badia's six-sided Romanesque campanile.

Leave the Badia and cross to the **Bargello** (Tuesday to Saturday 9am–2pm, Sunday 9am–1pm, closed Monday, 6,000 lire), begun in 1255 as the city's first town hall but later used as a court and prison as the names of the surrounding streets remind us (Via dei Malcontenti/Street of the Miserable, for example was the route

Bronze bird at the Bargello

taken from the Bargello to the gallows). The noble inner courtyard, where criminals were once tortured and executed, is now a peaceful spot whose walls are studded with *stelle* (carved armorial stones). The room on the right contains a rich collection of 16th-century sculpture; Michelangelo's first great work, the *Drunken Bacchus* (1499), seems to stagger off his pedestal.

A stately external staircase leads up to the first floor loggia where there is an amusing display of bronze birds made by Giambologna for the grotto of the Medicis' Villa di Castello (see *Option 7*).

The vast hall on the right, formerly the courtroom, contains Donatello's *St George* (1416), a puzzled, uneasy figure, alert to some unseen danger, which was commissioned by the Guild of Armourers for their nich on the exterior of Orsanmichele. Also here is the same sculptor's erotically charged *David* (1440), wearing not much more than an enigmatic smile. On the right-hand wall are the two trial panels made by Ghiberti and Brunelleschi, the winner and runner-up respectively in the competition of 1401 to find a designer for the Baptistry doors; both show the *Sacrifice of Isaac*.

The rest of this rich museum is a mixed bag covering everything from Islamic ceramics to coins and armour. Exploring at will you are bound to find something of interest; perhaps the 6th-century Lombardic jewellery or the rich Persian carpets on this floor, or the sculptures by Verrocchio on the floor above.

Leaving the Bargello, turn left and first left down Via della Vi-

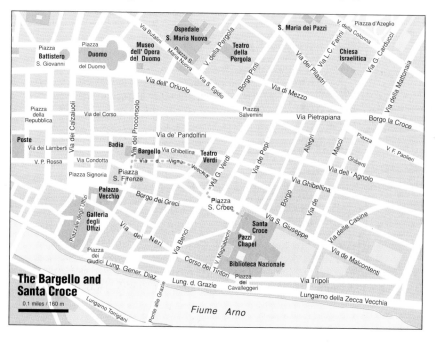

The Bargello and Santa Croce

0.1 miles / 160 m

Calcio festival, Piazza Santa Croce

gna Vecchia. At the second turning right look for the **Bar Vivoli Gelateria** (Via Isola delle Stinche 7r, closed Monday), a tiny ice-cream parlour that attracts huge crowds for its imaginative concoctions. Newspaper clippings posted on the wall carry rave reviews proclaiming this the home of the 'best ice-cream in the world'.

From here it is a short walk down Via de' Lavatoi, then right, into the huge square fronting **Santa Croce** (Monday to Saturday 7am–12.30pm and 3–6.30pm; Sunday 3–6pm), the magnificent Gothic burial place of many famous Florentines. On the right-hand side of the entrance door, heading up the aisle, you will find Michelangelo's tomb, carved by Vasari, Dante's empty sarcophagus (he refused to return to the city that sent him into exile and is actually buried in Ravenna), and the graves of Machiavelli, Leonardo Bruni, the humanist, and the composer, Rossini.

The Bardi Chapel (to the right of the high altar) is covered in frescos on the *Life of St Francis*, once thought to be by Giotto and now attributed to his pupil Taddeo Gaddi, father of Agnolo. The corridor on the right leads past the sacristy to a chapel containing Galileo's now empty grave (his body was moved to the north aisle of the church in 1737 when his contention that the sun, not the earth, was at the centre of the universe was no longer considered a heresy). The floor of the church is also covered in carved grave slabs.

Time to cool off?

Outside and to the left of the church is the entrance to the **Museo dell'Opera di Santa Croce** (Thursday to Tuesday, 10am–12.30pm and 2.30–6.30pm or 3–5pm in winter, closed Wednesday). Here you will be charmed by the quiet serenity of the two cloisters and amused by some of the 19th-century tombs that line the cloister walk; this leads to the **Pazzi Chapel**, a supremely noble building of white walls and contrasting grey *pietra serena* pilasters, designed by Brunelleschi. It is one of the purest works of the Renaissance.

Brunelleschi's Innocenti orphanage, Santissima Annunziata and the Archaeological Museum.

This morning tour takes in a clutch of little-visited museums and monuments in the north of the city. From Piazza del Duomo, head up Via dei Servi. The street is likely to be busy with traffic and the pavements crowded with Florentines heading for work, but do try to find a quiet doorway from which to admire some of Via dei Servi's imposing buildings.

At the first junction, note the **Palazzo Pucci** on the left, home of the Marchese Pucci and headquarters of his fashion empire. Further up on the left, at No 15, the **Palazzo Niccolini** (1550) is an appropriate headquarters for the Ministry of Public works – note the *sgraffito* decoration (designs scratched in plaster) and the huge overhanging roof sheltering an open loggia.

Via dei Servi leads into **Piazza della Santissima Annunziata**, one of the most beautiful squares in Florence, though cars and coaches detract from its visual harmony. In the centre of the square is an equestrian statue of Duke Ferdinand I, by Giambologna; it is partnered by two bronze fountains (by Tacca, 1608) featuring marine monsters and proving that the 20th century does not have a monopoly on bizarre fantasy creations.

On the right-hand side of the square is the gracious colonnade of the **Spedale degli Innocenti** built by Brunelleschi from 1419 and the very first classical loggia of its type. Here the elegant columns of grey *pietra serena* alternate harmoniously with Luca della Robbia's blue and white terracotta roundels depicting a baby in swaddling clothes – the symbol of the Innocenti orphanage which lies behind. The orphanage, the first in the world (opened in 1444), is still in operation. It has a small **gallery** of pictures donated by wealthy patrons, including Ghirlandaio's radiant *Adoration* (Monday to Saturday 9am–2pm, Sunday 8am–1pm, closed Wednesday, 3,000 lire).

Brunelleschi's portico was copied on the opposite side of the square, where it fronts the entrance to one of the best hotels in Florence, the Loggiata dei Serviti, and on the north side, where it forms the entrance to the church of

Romantic city

'The Chimera'

Santissima Annunziata (daily 7am–12.30pm and 4–7pm, admission free). This contains some outstanding frescos, including Andrea del Sarto's *Birth of the Virgin* (1514) and, in the adjacent Chiostro dei Morti (Cloister of the Dead), the same artist's *Holy Family*.

In the top right-hand corner of the square, at Via della Colonna 36, you will find the **Museo Archeologico**, the Archaeological Museum (Tuesday to Saturday 9am–2pm, Sunday 9am–1pm, closed Monday, 6,000 lire). Prominence here is given to a rich collection of ancient Egyptian material which resulted from a joint French-Italian expedition of 1889; it includes superbly well-preserved clothing and wooden furniture as well as a complete 14th-century BC chariot. The real stars of the museum, however, are the Etruscan bronzes in Room XIV. The 5th-century BC *Chimera* (pictured above), part lion, part goat and part snake, was discovered in Arezzo in 1554 and was greatly admired by Renaissance bronze-casters, including Benvenuto Cellini, who was entrusted with the restoration of a broken foreleg. The *Orator* (2nd century BC) was discovered in Trasimeno in 1556

Inside Santissima Annunziata

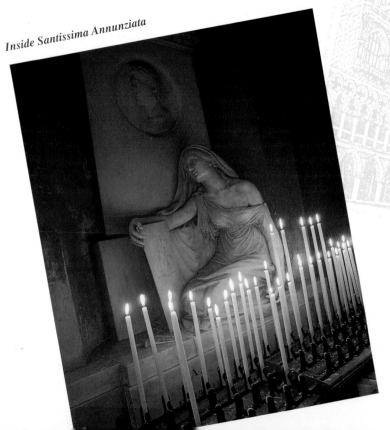

Option 3. The Museo dell'Opera del Duomo

Masterpieces of Gothic and Renaissance sculpture in wood, bronze and marble.

The **Museo dell'Opera del Duomo** (Cathedral Works Museum) is one of Florence's best small museums and it has the merit of long opening hours, so you can pop in whenever you have a spare moment – over lunch, perhaps, when much else is closed (Monday to Saturday 9am–7.30pm in summer, 9am–6pm in winter, closed Sunday, 6,000 lire). If you want a coffee and a snack first, try the **Gran Caffe**, Piazza San Giovanni 1r, directly opposite the south doors of the Baptistry on Piazza del Duomo – a chic coffee bar with colourful fresco fragments on the wall.

Thus fortified, turn right out of the café and walk along the south flank of the Duomo, passing Giotto's campanile, and bearing left round the east end of the cathedral. Look out for an archway on the right, with the bust of Duke Cosimo I above – No 9 Piazza del Duomo – and enter the courtyard of the museum. It was here, between 1501 and 1504, that Michelangelo carved his mighty statue of *David*. The courtyard is now decorated with baroque sculptures and Roman sarcophagi. The building that houses the museum was the office of the Cathedral Workshop, established in the 15th century to maintain the fabric of the cathedral and commission new works. Today it houses numerous sculptural works, principally from the cathedral exterior, brought indoors to protect them against pollution and weathering.

Michelangelo's 'Pietà'

The first room contains displays on the construction of the cathedral dome and examples of the pulleys, capstans and winches used by 15th-century labourers. Another room contains sculptures intended for the cathedral facade, which didn't get completed until the 19th century. Most striking of the figures is Donatello's *St John the Evangelist*; compare this with Ciuffagni's *St Matthew* – clearly an attempt to imitate Donatello's style.

The mezzanine floor is devoted to a single work – Michelangelo's *Pietà*, begun around 1550 and originally intended for his own tomb. The tall hooded figure at the centre of the group is a self-portrait – Michelangelo cast himself as Nicodemus, the rich man who donated his tomb for the

14th-century panel in the museum

burial of Christ. The rather stiff and inferior carving of Mary Magdalene, to the left, is by one of Michelangelo's pupils. The great master himself broke up the sculpture, dissatisfied with his work, and it survived only because a servant kept the pieces.

On the first floor of the museum are two superb *cantorie*, choir galleries, carved in marble, which were removed from the cathedral in the 17th century. Both depict young musicians in a joyous frenzy of dancing, singing and cymbal-crashing. They were made by two of the leading artists of the day, Donatello and Luca della Robbia, between 1431 and 1438. Here, too, you will find Donatello's powerful *Mary Magdalene*, a figure of penitence carved in wood, her features haggard from fasting and grief.

Discussing the next move

Beyond, a whole room is devoted to the panels that once adorned the base of Giotto's campanile, some designed by Giotto, others by Andrea Pisano. Amongst a number of subjects celebrating human knowledge, they depict various trades, showing in vivid detail what the workshop of a sculptor or artist would have looked like in the 14th century.

In the last room of the museum, Lorenzo Ghiberti's original bronze panels from the Paradise (east) door of the Baptistry are displayed – some are already here and others are still being restored. They provide an admirable opportunity for visitors to study in close-up the work that has come to stand as a symbol of the birth of the Renaissance.

The Room of the Parrots, Palazzo Davanzati

Option 4. The Palazzo Davanzati

Step inside this beautiful palace for a taste of life in Renaissance Florence before exploring nearby medieval alleys.

Start at the **Palazzo Davanzati**, Via Porta Rossa 13, also known as the **Museo dell'Antica Casa Fiorentina** (Tuesday–Saturday 9am–2pm, Sunday 9am–1pm, closed Monday, 6,000 lire).

Look at the facade first; this dates to the mid-14th century and is a typical example of Tuscan pre-Renaissance architecture. You will see plenty of buildings like this in Siena and other Tuscan cities, but in Florence it is a rarity because of the huge amount of rebuilding that went on from the 15th century. A typical feature is the so-called depressed arch over the doors and windows. The coat of arms is that of the Davanzati family who owned the palace from 1518 until 1538. The open loggia that crowns the palace was added in the 16th century.

Inside is a very beautiful courtyard and an elegant stone staircase supported on flying arches. Note, too, the well to the right of the entrance with its pulley system enabling buckets of water to be lifted to each of the five floors of the palace – having a private water supply was a considerable luxury, since most Florentines were dependent on the water supplied by public fountains, which needed fetching and carrying by bucket.

The principal living-rooms lie on the first floor, the *piano nobile*, where you will find the gorgeously frescoed dining-room, known as the **Sala dei Papagalli** (Room of the Parrots) after the birds pictured in the borders. The bedchambers on the floors above have similar murals, notably the room on the second floor, which is decorated with scenes from the 13th-century French romance, the *Châtelaine de Vergy*. Though the contemporary furnishings in each room, consisting of beds, chests and stools, may look sparse,

BENVENUTO CELLINI

ESCLUSO

they represent a considerable degree of luxury for the time, as do the private bathrooms off each room, complete with toilets and terracotta waste pipes. The kitchen is located on the top floor, so that smoke and cooking smells would not permeate the living-rooms. Here, too, you will find a fascinating array of contemporary utensils, including equipment for kneading and shaping pasta.

As you leave the palace, look opposite and to the left to see the remains of a medieval tower-house that is typical of an even earlier, medieval, style of architecture. Turn right and first right again, in Via Pellicheria, to reach another well-preserved group of medieval structures, the battlemented buildings of the **Palazzo di Parte Guelfa**. This dates to the 13th century and was aesthetically enhanced by Vasari, who built the external staircase in the 16th century. This palace once served as the headquarters of the Guelf party, one of the political factions whose feuding caused mayhem in the city during the 13th and 14th centuries.

Walk through the tunnel straight ahead and turn right in Via delle Terme (commemorating the former site of the Roman baths) with its narrow medieval alleys leading off to the left. Take the second left, Via del Fiordaliso, noting the huge stone *sporti*, or brackets, of the building to the right, supporting the jettied-out upper storeys. Turn right, then first left into **Piazza del Limbo**, so called because the site was once used as a graveyard for unbaptised infants whose souls, according to the prevailing dogma, could not enter heaven and dwelled in Limbo. The church on the left, **Santi Apostoli**, is one of the oldest in the city, dating to around 1050. It incorporates Corinthian columns salavaged from the Roman baths.

Turn left in Borgo Sante Apostoli and cross the busy **Piazza di Santa Trinità** to the church of the same name (daily 7am–noon and 4–7pm, admission free). Here the relative austerity of the 13th-century Gothic architecture contrasts with Ghirlandaio's stunningly colourful frescos and altarpiece of the **Sassetti Chapel**, to the right of the choir. The frescos (1483) illustrate the *Life of St Francis* and the altarpiece (1485) shows the *Nativity*. Other frescos depict scenes from classical writing and mythology set against a Florentine backdrop, suggesting that Renaissance Florence was conceived as being the new Rome.

This somewhat strenuous walk to the jewel-like church of San Miniato and the Piazzale Michelangelo is rewarded by sweeping views down over the rooftops of Florence.

The lovely Romanesque church of San Miniato al Monte sits on a hill to the south of the city and Florentines like to head up here for their Sunday afternoon walk. You can, of course, visit any day of the week, timing your walk to coincide with the church opening hours (daily 8am–noon and 2.30–7pm or 6pm in winter), admission free).

From **Piazza della Signoria**, walk south through the courtyard of the Uffizi gallery to the Arno embankment and turn left. As you follow the river, look up to the right where you will see the green and white marble facade of San Miniato. The view across the Arno to this church was celebrated in E M Forster's novel, *A Room With a View* – the room concerned was located in the Pensione Simi (now the Jennings-Riccioli hotel). When you reach the first bridge, the Ponte alle Grazie, the hotel stands a little further up on the left-hand side.

In the Piazzale Michelangelo

Cross the bridge and take the third left, Via di San Miniato. This leads you through an arch in the 14th-century city wall, where you turn left in Via dei Bastioni.

Keep left and then look for a set of stone steps on the right which leads straight uphill, interrupted every so often by the main road, passing through leafy gardens. When the staircase stops, turn right along the road and look for a gate on the left leading into the **Giardino delle Rose**, or Rose Garden (9am–7pm, admission free). There is much more to see here than just roses and plant-lovers will delight in the colourful profusion. Follow the path through the garden and, at the exit gates, climb the steps to the right to reach the **Piazzale**

Souvenirs

Michelangelo. This viewpoint was laid out in the 19th century and the broad square is dotted with reproductions of Michelangelo's celebrated sculptures – not to mention scores of tour buses and numerous souvenir stalls. The views, though, are marvellous – it is from here that all those classic postcard pictures of the rooftops of Florence are taken.

Turning your back on the Piazzale, head for the **Bar/Ristorante La Loggia**, housed in a 19th-century neoclassical building, where you may want to stop for lunch. If not, keep to the right of the restaurant, then take the flight of steps to the left which leads up to the church of San Salvatore. Follow the path to the right of this church, then take the left-most road towards an arch in the wall surrounding **San Miniato** and its conventual buildings. Catch your breath while admiring the views from the terrace in front of the church and studying its delicate facade, covered in geometric patterns of green and white marble.

The church was built on the site of the tomb of the city's first Christian martyr, St Minias. He was executed in AD250 during the anti-Christian purges of the Emperor Diocletian and his shrine was replaced by the present church in AD1018. It incorporates Corinthian columns and other Roman materials. Important features inside are the intarsia panels of the floor, now worn, depicting signs of the zodiac, the numerous fragments of 11th- and 12th-century Byzantine-style frescos on the walls, and the raised marble choir and pulpit inset with intarsia panels and depicting mythical beasts. To the left, behind an iron grille, is the tomb of the Cardinal of Portugal who died on a visit to Florence in 1439. The mosaic in the apse, of 1297, shows **Christ, the Virgin and St Minias**.

With your back to the church façade, descend the stone staircase opposite, passing through the cemetery and noting the fine 19th-century sculptures marking some of the graves. Cross the road,

The view from Piazzale Michelangelo

continue down the next set of steps, cross the road at the bottom and bear right to find Via del Monte alle Croci on the left. Follow this winding road downhill until you return to the arch in the city wall. A little café to the left (the **Fuori Porta**) has a quiet sunny terrace for enjoying coffee or ice-cream. You can now retrace your earlier steps to the city centre, or turn left to follow Via di Belvedere. This involves an uphill climb, following the foot of the city walls, until you reach Porta San Giorgio, built in 1260 and the city's oldest surviving gate.

Alongside the gate is an entrance to the **Forte Belvedere** (daily 9am–8pm in summer, to 7pm in winter, admission free) which you can enter for more sweeping views of the city before descending through the Boboli Gardens (see *Day 3, page 42*). Alternatively, pass through the Porta San Giorgio and descend the quiet Costa San Giorgio, noting No 19 which stands on the site of Galileo's home. Where the road forks, take the left-hand route to reach Piazza Santa Felicità, just a few steps from the Ponte Vecchio and the north bank.

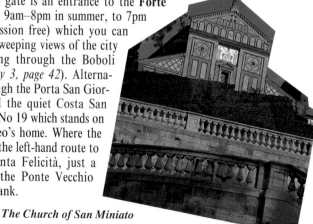

The Church of San Miniato

Option 6. Fiesole

Escape to the hills for a walk and lunch in the sleepy village that stands less than 4 miles/6km from the centre of Florence.

Fiesole is a favourite retreat for Florentines who find the air in this hilltop village fresher and cooler than in the valley bottom where their own city sits. Once, relations between Florence and Fiesole were not so comfortable. Fiesole predates Florence by some eight centuries; it was an Etruscan city well before the Romans colonised the area and founded the town from which Florence grew. Thereafter Fiesole declined but remained an important trade competitor to Florence until 1125 when Florentine troops stormed Fiesole, destroying all the buildings, save for the cathedral.

From the 15th century many fine villas were built on the slopes leading up to Fiesole. They were rented by a growing Anglo community which included – from the 19th century – poets Robert and Elizabeth Barrett Browning. You will see these villas from the bus as you approach Fiesole – take bus No 7 from **Santa Maria Novella** station, buying your ticket in advance from one of the ticket machines located on the pavement alongside the bus stop. The 30-minute journey ends at the **Piazza Mino**, Fiesole's broad main square which occupies the site of the Roman forum.

Cross the square to find the entrance to the **Teatro Romano** (daily 9am–7pm in summer, 10am–4pm in winter, 5,000 lire).

This impeccably preserved amphitheatre, with a seating capacity of 3,000, is the site of a summer arts festival held in July and August (*see page 80*).

It enjoys stunning views over the low, cypress-topped hills of the rural Mugello region to the north. Surrounding the theatre are the jumbled remains of Etruscan and Roman temples and baths. The excellent **Museum Faesulanum**, within the same complex, displays tiny Etruscan figures (dancers, warriors,-orators); sensual (but headless) statues of Dionysos and Venus and a variety of other interesting sculptures.

Almost opposite the Teatro Romano entrance, in Via

Dupre, the **Museo Bandini** has an interesting collection of paintings, furniture, majolica and Byzantine carved ivories (daily 10am–noon and 3–7pm in summer, 10am–12.30pm and 2.30–6pm in winter, 4,000 lire).

Back on the Piazza Mino, turn right to the rather forbidding and over-restored **Duomo** (cathedral). Look for Via San Francesco, the lane that climbs steeply from the cathedral facade. Pass **Sant'Alessandro**, whose plain, squat facade hides a 6th-century basilica with re-used Roman columns of *cipollino* (onion-ring) marble, to **San Francesco**, seated on the site of an Etruscan temple. There are lovely views from the terrace halfway up. Since the 15th century it has been a monastery and a friendly monk will allow you entry to go upstairs and inspect the barren cells in which these holy men spent most of their lives.

You can now reward your exertions by having lunch at one of the restaurants in Piazza Mino or, if you prefer, by simply enjoying a drink and the fine views from the terrace of the lovely Hotel Villa Aurora.

Mixed facade of the Badia Fiesolana

You can now return to Florence by bus or walk part of the way, following the narrow Via Vecchia Fiesolana out of the square. Along the way you will pass the **Villa Medici**, built in 1458, a favourite retreat of Lorenzo de'Medici, as well as enjoy glimpses of other villas behind their high walls and note various examples of stone work, a fountain, lions' heads and sentinel cypress trees.

The next stop on the route, after ½ mile (1km), is the **convent of San Domenico** where you can see Fra Angelico's *Madonna with Angels* (1430) in the church and his *Crucifixion* (1430) in the Chapter House.

From here, you can take the left fork down to the **Badia Fiesolana**, the church that served as Fiesole's cathedral until 1058. Its original Romanesque facade, which is framed by the rough, unfinished stonework of the enlarged 15th-century church, is a delicate work of inlaid marble. There is another magnificent view over Florence to be enjoyed from the terrace in front of the church.

Back at the Convent of San Domenico, the right-hand road will eventually lead you back down to the main road where the No 7 bus stops on the way back to Florence.

A visit to two Medici villas with fine gardens in the northern suburbs of the city.

This tour is a must for garden-lovers – but don't expect colourful herbaceous borders: the two gardens we will visit today were laid out in the formal Italian style in the 16th century, and are of great historical interest. They are open all day, every day except Monday, and can be enjoyed in all seasons. The garden of the Villa della Petreia is backed by extensive woodland which is perfect for picnicking.

Take bus 28A, B or C from the stop to the extreme right of the **Santa Maria Novella** bus station. Buses leave every 15 minutes or so and tickets can be bought from the machine by the bus-stop.

Knowing where to get off the bus is going to be the most difficult part of this tour – befriend someone on the bus, if possible, and ask them to tell you where to get off for the Villa Medicea della Petreia. Alternatively, keep an eye on the street signs – the bus heads north to the suburb of Rifredi, then follows the railway track along the long Via Reginaldo Giuliani. After about 15 minutes you will pass a power station on the right just before Via Reginaldo Giuliani narrows down to a single lane. Count the house numbers on the right – you want to get out at the request stop outside house No 424.

Lurking figure, Villa di Castello

From there, walk back to house No 292 and turn left up the narrow Via della Petreia. About ⅓ mile/0.5km up the lane you will pass the Villa Corsini, with its cream-coloured baroque facade and a plaque recording that Robert Dudley died here on September 6, 1649. Dudley, the illegitimate son of the Earl of Leicester (Queen Elizabeth I's favourite) was the leading marine engineer of his age and was employed by Cosimo I to build the harbour at Livorno, Tuscany's principal port.

The **Villa della Petreia** is another ⅔ mile/1km up from here (Tuesday to Saturday 9am–7.30pm, but closing earlier in winter, Sunday 9am–1.30pm, closed Monday, admission free).

Enter the gate and take the first entrance in the wall on the right, passing into the garden that fronts the villa, laid out with low box hedges enclosing flower beds. Take the central path up steps and past a large fish tank to the terrace in front of the villa. From here the scroll work and geometric patterning of the box parterre can best be appreciated. There is a good view from here left to the

Villa della Petreia

dome of Florence cathedral, straight ahead to the new industrial suburb of Firenze Nuova and right to the city's Peretola airport.

Tours of the villa itself are only given to groups of 10, so you may have to wait and team up with other visitors (then press the bell to the right of the entrance). The main sight inside is the central hallway, covered in frescos on the history of the Medici. The villa itself was built in 1575 for Grand Duke Ferdinand I, on the site of an earlier fortress, whose tower is still preserved. During the 19th century Villa della Petreia was the favourite residence of the King of Italy, Victor Emmanuel II and it was he who had the tree house built in the huge (and now dead) ilex oak to the left of the villa facade.

To the right of the villa, a gate in the wall leads to a large park full of ilex and cypress trees, dense enough to be cool even in the heat of summer and threaded with little streams. This juxtaposition of the very formal garden with wild and mysterious woodland was a favourite device of Italian gardeners.

From the Villa della Petreia, return downhill to the Villa Corsini and turn right, down Via di Castello. Follow this road, ignoring all side turnings, and you will find the **Villa di Castello** on the right after ⅓ mile/0.5km (open Tuesday–Sunday 9am–7.30pm, but closing earlier in winter, closed Monday, admission free).

Turn left at the rear of the villa (not open to the public) to reach the formal garden, laid out for Duke Cosimo I in 1541 and once regarded as the supreme example of Renaissance gardening – for the Grand Tourists of the 18th and 19th century, this was a compulsory sight. It now lacks some of the features that made it famous – at the back of the garden, the shell-encrusted **Grotta degli Animali** (1579) was once filled with the delightful bronze birds of Giambologna, since moved to the Bargello Museum (see *Option 1, page 46*). Even so, the geometric beds, outlined in box, and the rows of huge terracotta pots containing citrus trees and bougainvillaea are very striking and, viewed from the upper terrace, resemble a vast patterned carpet.

Once again, the ordered formality of the parterre contrasts with the wilder woodland above, where the shivering figure of Appennino (by Ammanati) rises from a pool.

To return to Florence, exit from the villa and walk down the avenue directly opposite. Cross Via Peginalio Giuliani and continue down Via Fiulio Bechi. Cross the next road, Via Sestesi, and look for the bus-stop a short way down on the right.

Flow with the crowds on an early evening stroll around the city, taking in the principal shops.

The *passeggiata*, or evening promenade, is a traditional feature of Italian life. From about 6pm, as people finish their work for the day, everyone pours out onto the central streets of Florence. There they stroll arm-in-arm to do some last-minute shopping, stopping to greet old friends and gossip, or they stand in conspiratorial groups to discuss appropriate issues in business, politics or the latest *cause célèbre*.

Watching other people is all part of the fun and in Florence – where locals and foreign visitors intermingle – it is not hard to spot the true Florentines because of the way they dress; looking good (*fare bella figura*) is a matter in which they take pride. As you join the crowds we will note some of the main shops of central Florence, whose attractive window-displays act as punctuation marks along the way – you may be tempted to fit yourself out with a set of smart new clothes so as to look as much as possible like an honorary Florentine.

Begin you stroll in **Piazza del Duomo** and head south down Via Calzaiuoli. The first shop on the right, **Armando Poggi** (103r), stocks kitchenware and china, from classic designs to ultra-modern; this is the place where wealthy young Florentines place their wedding lists.

Further down, at **Migone** (85r), you can buy little hand-painted boxes and fill them with a selection of chocolates, bon-bons, marzipan fruits or sweet biscuits. A little way down on the left, **Ceramiche Calzaiuoli** (80r) is packed to the ceiling with reproduction Renaissance majolica and more modern pieces, everything from small tiles to huge jars and bowls.

Ready for a promenade

Also on the left, **Coin** (56r) is a fashionable galleria, selling chic own-label clothing that does not cost the earth. By contrast **Beltrami** (both sides of the street, 44r and 31r) is at the high-cost end of the fashion market. From these two shops Beltrami first began selling the shoes, clothing and leather goods that are now renowned throughout Italy.

Ice-creams coming up: **Perche Noi** (meaning 'Why Not?') is one of the oldest and best *gelati* makers in the city; the little shop is on the left, just after Beltrami, at Via dei Tavolini 19r. On the right, just at the entrance to Piazza della Signoria, is **Pineider**

Mask at Firenze of Papier Mâché

(13r); stop to admire the hand-printed stationery, albums, prints and leather briefcases. Well-bred Italians, heads of state and Hollywood film stars have their personalised stationery printed here. This city is well-known for its paper products.

Turn right in Via Caccherec-cia, past the **Erboristeria** (Herbalist) at No 9r, with its frescoed and beamed interior. Turn left in Via Por Santa Maria and follow the crowds to Ponte Vecchio. Apart from the numerous jewellers' shops, you may well find buskers and street traders on the bridge (keeping a wary eye out for the police). Be wary yourself of any bargains that seem too good to be true.

The crowd pushes on south down Via Guicciardini. Follow the flow and look out for **Del Secco** (20r) selling lace and hand-embroidered linen, and **Giulio Giannini e Figlio** (37r) where you can buy marbled papers, notepads, albums and paper sculpture. In Piazza dei Pitti, **Pitti Mosaici** (16r) keeps alive the ancient Florentine art of making tables with *trompe-l'oeuil* designs out of inlaid marble and semi-precious stones; you can also buy more portable items, such as jewellery. A little way beyond this, **Firenze of Papier Mâché** (10r) makes everything from traditional carnival masks to enormous painted murals.

At this point turn back and swim against the flow of human bodies to reach Piazza della Signoria. Now take a seat and a well-earned rest at **Rivoire**, the café with the best view of the square. Relax and watch the buskers, the crowds, the pigeons and the horse-drawn carriages over a rich cup of iced chocolate and, if you have any money left, take away a tiny box of Rivoire's delectable handmade chocolates as a souvenir.

Florence is famous for its marbled paper

Option 9. Excursion to Pisa

Visit the world-famous Leaning Tower, the cathedral, Baptistry and Camposanto on a day trip from Florence.

Many visitors to Florence arrive and depart from Pisa's Galileo Galilei airport, but never find time to visit Pisa itself. This is a pity, since Pisa is very easy to reach from Florence and its sights are memorable. Trains for Pisa depart from **Santa Maria Novella** station in Florence every hour every day of the week and the fare is very cheap.

The train follows the Arno valley downstream, calling first at the industrial town of Empoli, before arriving at Pisa Centrale station after 53 minutes. Alight here and exit the station, heading straight up Viale Gramsci, crossing the busy Piazza Vittorio Emanuele and continuing up Corso Italia.

This brings you to the banks of the Arno river, much wider here than in Florence and bridged by the Ponte di Mezzo. Cross to Piazza Garibaldi and walk up the arcaded Borgo Stretto, Pisa's animated main shopping street. Take the first left, Via Dini, to reach the **Piazza dei Cavalieri**.

This square is dominated by the Palazzo della Carovana, built by Vasari in 1562 and covered in black and white *sgraffiti* decoration. The palazzo stands on the site of Pisa's original town hall, demolished in 1509 to symbolise the subjugation of Pisa after the city had been defeated by the Florentines.

A large and domineering statue of Duke Cosimo I stands in front of the palace. To the right of the palace is the church of Santo Stefano which contains war trophies captured by the crusading *cavalieri* (knights) of St Stephen in battles with the Turks. To the left is the grim Torre Gualandi, known as the Tower of Hunger, where Count Ugolino, along with all his sons and grandsons, was walled up and starved to death in 1288 for allegedly betraying Pisa to the Genoese – the story is told in Dante's *Inferno* (Canto XXXIII) and Shelley's poem, *The Tower of Famine*.

Pass under the arch beneath the clock tower of the Palazzo dell'Orologia, to the left, and take the right-hand street, Via Martiri. This bends left to join Via San Giuseppe, which leads to the **Campo dei Miracoli** (Field of Miracles) where the bizarre ensemble of Pisa's Leaning Tower, cathedral and Baptistry is revealed.

No matter how many photographs you may have seen, nothing

The Leaning Tower with Pisa's Duomo or cathedral

The Duomo's facade dates from 1063

prepares you for the impact of these extraordinary buildings seen at first hand. Pisa was a thriving port until the mouth of the River Arno silted up, and the city had extensive trade contacts with Spain and North Africa during the 12th and 13th centuries – hence the Moorish influence on the architecture of these idiosyncratic buildings, clearly evident in the marble arabesque patterns that cover the walls of the cathedral and the bristling, minaret-like pinnacles of the Baptistry. All of the buildings tilt – not just the Leaning Tower; hence the effect of vertigo you are likely to experience if you look too long.

The **Leaning Tower**, begun in 1173, started to tilt during the early stages of construction, when it was only 35-ft (10.5-metre) high (some people say the Pisans deliberately built it this way so as to ensure a healthy income from tourism). Completed in 1350, the tower has continued to slide, so that now, 180-ft (54.5-metre) high, it leans 15ft (4.5 metre) from the perpendicular. It is likely that the tower will be supported by scaffolding when you visit: to prevent further subsidence, an ambitious 300-billion-lire programme of underpinning was embarked upon in 1991 that will take several years to complete.

The **Duomo** (cathedral) alongside is as interesting for its exterior as its interior. It was begun in 1063 and the facade is covered in rising tiers of colonnades, typical of the distinctive Pisan Romanesque style. The bronze doors below these colonnades date to 1602 and illustrate biblical scenes. The cathedral is entered through the south transept which also has important Romanesque bronze doors, designed by Bonnano da Pisa in 1180 and illustrating scenes from the *Life of Christ*.

Fire devastated the interior in 1595 but spared Cimabue's mosaic of *Christ in Majesty* (1302) in the vault of the apse and Giovanni Pisano's outstanding pulpit carved with New Testament scenes. The work of the father-and-son team, Nicola and Giovanni Pisano, transcends art historical categories. Though working in the 13th century, when Gothic was the predominant style, their output anticipates the best Renaissance sculpture of the next century. You will see more of it in the Baptistry, which was designed and completed by the Pisani in 1284 and contains Nicola Pisano's fine pulpit, carved with animated scenes from the *Life of Christ*.

Vasari tells us that the Pisani were influenced by the carvings on the Roman sarcophagi that are to be found in the **Camposanto** (Holy Field) cemetery that lies to the north of the cathedral, enclosed by marble walls. This was begun in 1278, and shiploads of soil were brought back from the Holy Land, along with the sarcophagi, in Pisan ships to add sanctity to the burial ground. The cloister walls surrounding the cemetery were once gloriously frescoed, but they were seriously damaged when a stray Allied bomb hit the cemetery in 1944. Even so, fragments remain of a lively *Last Judgment* by an unknown 14th-century artist.

On the opposite side of the Campo dei Miracoli is the **Museo delle Sinopie**, to which the remaining frescos of the Camposanto have been removed. Many of them consist of nothing more than the *sinopie*, preliminary designs sketched into the plaster undercoat to guide the artist during the final stage – painting the finished fresco on to the moist final coat of plaster.

Perhaps more interesting is the **Museo dell'Opera del Duomo** on the corner of the Piazza del Duomo nearest to the Leaning Tower. This contains numerous works of art, including Giovanni Pisano's exquisite *Virgin and Child* carved in ivory, and there is an unusual view of the Leaning Tower to be had from the museum courtyard.

From Piazza del Duomo, take Via Roma southwards, passing the Orto Botanico (Botanical Garden) until you reach the Arno embankment. Turn right along Lungarno Simonelli and cross the next bridge. Turn left to reach the church of **San Paolo a Ripa d'Arno**, with another splendid Pisan Romanesque facade. Further down the Arno embankment is the extraordinary church of **Santa Maria della Spina**, covered in prickly pinnacles and niches containing statues of the Virgin, Christ and the Apostles. This 14th-century Gothic church was built to house a thorn from the Crown of Thorns, a theme picked up in the bristling exterior architecture.

A right turn here will take you down Via Sant'Antonio and back to Pisa Centrale station, from where hourly trains depart for Florence.

Santa Maria della Spina

Shopping

Some visitors come to Florence simply to shop – never mind the monuments. To be this indulgent, it is better to be affluent, of course. For those of lesser means, window-shopping can be almost as much fun, and there are genuine bargains to be found if you search diligently enough, especially in the big street markets around San Lorenzo and the Mercato Nuovo.

High fashion in Via de' Tornabuoni

Although Milan claims to be the world capital of *haute couture*, Florence has its fair share of homegrown designers of international repute. Nearly all have their outlets at the southern end of Via de' Tornabuoni, the upmarket shopping area. The exception is Emilio Pucci, famous for his sexy underwear and for inventing the trouser suit (known as palazzo pyjamas when trouser suits were all the rage as evening wear in the 1960s). The Marchese Pucci lives in an ancestral palace, designed by Ammanati, at Via de' Pucci 6;

here you will find the Pucci boutique, while the shop around the corner (Via Ricasoli 20r) sells Chianti Classico wines, Vinsanto and olive oil produced on the Pucci estates.

A tour of Via de' Tornabuoni should start on the eastern (even-numbered) side of the road. **Ugolini** (20-22r) sells gloves that are almost softer than skin. At **Bijoux Casciou** (32r) the speciality is costume jewellery.

At the bottom of the street (16r), in the 13th-century Palazzo Spini-Ferroni, is the boutique of **Salvatore Ferragamo** who, whilst working in Hollywood, became known as the 'shoemaker to the stars'. The family-run firm now sells clothing, luggage and relatively inexpensive silk scarves and ties,

Stationery for sale

as well as the famous footwear.

Across on the west side of the road are rival shoemakers, **Casadei** (33r) and **Tanino Crisci** (43-45r). Then comes **Valentino** (67r); the jeweller **Mario Buccellati** (72r) and, last of all, the flagship store of **Gucci**.

The next street left, Via della Vigna Nuova, is now almost an extension of Via de' Tornabuoni. Here you will find brightly coloured fashions at **Enrico Coveri** (27-29r) and **Naj Oleari** (35r). Equally fun are the woven baskets, hats, furniture and sculptures at **Emilio Paoli** (26r). **Giorgio Armani** is a little further down (51r) and if, by now, you have had enough of clothes, go and see the period photographs on show at **Alinari** (46–48r).

Food, fashion and fabrics in the city centre

Just to the east of Piazza del Duomo, at Via dei Vecchietta 28r, is the **Old England Stores**, a long narrow shop lined with glass-fronted cabinets selling everything from breakfast cereals and Fortnum & Mason marmalade to cashmeres and tweed. Its existence bears witness to the fact that some Florentines hold certain British products in high regard – but it is also surprising how many British holidaymakers come here.

Heading east towards Piazza del Duomo, do not miss **Casa dei Tessuti** at Via de' Pecori 20-24r; this textile shop is piled to the ceiling with costly antique-style fabrics, rich enough to grace a Renaissance palace.

By contrast, **Max Mara** opposite (23r) is full of bold but stylishly tailored modern clothes. Turn right down Via Roma for **Luisa** (71r), a large boutique that stocks clothes designed by the likes of Issey Miyake, Comme des Garçons, Jean-Paul Gaultier, along with many others. **Eredi Chianini** opposite (18-22r) is a very masculine shop, selling everything from jeans and aftershave to silk underwear and suits.

Further down, **Gilli**, on the right (3r) is renowned for its handmade chocolates and perfect pastries. Fronting Piazza della Repubblica, it is a chic spot for a drink or coffee; sitting outside doubles the tariff. Nearby, on the opposite left-hand side of the piazza, is the UPIM department store, a good place to shop if you cannot afford the high prices in the boutiques: it is opposite the classy Savoy Hotel.

Heading down Via Calimala, you will soon come to the crowded **Mercato Nuovo**, built in 1547 and packed with stalls selling leather goods, lace, costume jewellery, baskets and T-shirts. You can find some cheap and joky souvenirs here – a plastic illuminated model

Souvenir-seller rests her feet

of Michelangelo's *David* perhaps?

Alternatively, look for inexpensive soaps, pot pourri, perfumes and fragrances at the **Erboristeria della Antica Farmacia del Cinghiale** (Via Calimala 4r) alongside the market.

Going for Gold

Jewellers have been operating from the Ponte Vecchio since the 16th century. Unfortunately, much of what is sold on the bridge today is mass-produced in factories elsewhere and geared to the (affluent) tourist's desire for an appropriate souvenir. Charms and trinkets predominate. Some of the more interesting and creative jewellers on the bridge are:

Bijoux Cascio (Via Por Santa Maria 1r) which proves that not everything that glistens here is made of solid gold: this shop sells good chunky (gold-plated) modern jewellery at affordable prices; on the left-hand side of the bridge, look for the glittering display in the window of **Ristori** (if you need to ask the price, this shop is probably not for you). **U. Gherardi** is cheaper and specialises in coral and cultured pearls;

Piccini is one of the more imaginative jewellers on the bridge but also sells antique pieces.

On the opposite side of the bridge, you may see crowds outside **Cassetti's**, a shop whose contemporary designs attract admiring Florentines.

Melli sells only antique pieces – not

Jewellery for sale on Ponte Vecchio

just jewellery, but also silver snuff boxes, candlesticks, jugs and plates. **Rajola** is another affordable jeweller selling gold-plated pieces, set with semi-precious stones, plus elegant watches.

Food and drink

These shops off the beaten track are the best in their class and worth seeking out. **Alessi**, Via dell' Oche 29r, sells the widest selection of chocolates, biscuits, Tuscan honey and jams, wines and spirits that you will find in Florence. The drinks section alone is a delightful showcase for local wines, spirits and liqueurs; here you can still buy traditional straw-wrapped flasks of Chianti, and the *grappa vecchia* produced by Jacopo Poli is worth buying just for the elegance of the bottle designs.

If you have time, turn right out of Alessi, down to the end of Via dell' Oche, to find more gastronomic treats at **Pegna** (Via della Studio 28r) – the place to buy olive oil, balsamic vinegar, sun-dried tomatoes, dried mushrooms and bottled *antipasti*.

Fonte dei Dolci (Via Nazionale) is a fairlyland for those with a sweeth tooth. Slabs of chocolate in pink, orange, white or green; piles and bundles of brightly coloured packets of candies; nougat, marzipan, chocolate liqueurs, and everything beautiful enough to be a special gift.

Tempting pastries

Marbled paper

For marbled papers and patterned papers, a Florentine speciality, the best selection and keenest prices are to be found at **Bottega Artigiana del Libro**, Lungarno Corsini 40r, and shops opposite the Pitti Palace. Here you can buy sheets of paper, albums, notebooks, carnival masks and paper formed into delicate origami peacocks and flowers. While you are here do not miss **P. Bazzanti**, almost next door at 46r. This art gallery stocks bronze and marble reproductions of many Florentine statues – just the place to buy a nymph or deity for the garden.

Markets

Apart from Mercato Nuovo mentioned earlier, the big open-air market in the streets around San Lorenzo and around the Mercato Centrale has splendid bargains in leather goods, woollen jumpers, gloves, shoes and boots. It's hard to bargain with a Florentine, but try it. A flea market operates every day except Sunday at Piazza dei Ciompi, near Santa Croce. Great bargains here.

A Ponte Vecchio to take home

Eating Out

You can eat very well and cheaply in Florence on pizza and pasta, or on a simple diet put together from the offerings of street markets or an *alimentare* (grocer). On some occasions absolutely nothing can beat a picnic of bread (*pane*), plump black olives (*olive*), tomatoes (*pomodore*), sheep's cheese (*pecorino*), Tuscan ham (*prosciutto*) and fruits such as figs, apricots or peaches (*fichi, albicocche, pesce*).

Other occasions and other moods demand a full-blown meal in the Italian style, preferably *al fresco*, in a restaurant with a garden, since eating out in Italy is as much a social event as a gourmet experience. Everybody should try the Florentine speciality, *bistecca alla fiorentina*, at least once, despite the cost (the price on the menu is per unit (*etto*) of 100 grammes of raw meat. You can ask for it to be cooked rare (*al sangue*) or well-done (*ben cotta*). The result is a tender, juicy, rib steak, from cattle raised in the Val di Chiana, grilled over charcoal, fragrant with herbs and served with chunks of lemon.

Don't be afraid of 'fixed price' meals because they are usually good value for money. Check out Italian-style fast food places which offer pasta, pizza and vegetables as a change from hamburgers.

Basic rules

If you decide to eat in a *ristorante* or a *trattoria* you will be expected to order a first course (*prima*) of pasta, rice (*risotto*) or soup (*minestra*), followed by a main course (*secondo*) of meat or fish. This is served without accompaniment; if you want salad (*insalata*) or vegetables, you will have to order additional side dishes (*contorni*). The meal finishes with either fruit (*frutta*), cheese (*formaggio*), dessert (*dolci*) or ice-cream (*gelato*), followed by a coffee (*caffe* – invariably an *espresso*, unless you request otherwise). No meal would be complete unless partnered by the fruity red wines of Chianti (if you prefer white, try Vernaccio di San Gimignano), while for a final *digestive*, try Vinsanto, a sweet but complex dessert wine.

Prices

The price categories quoted below are based on the average cost of a three-course meal for two, including cover and service charges, but excluding the cost of drink: $ = up to 80,000 lire, $$ = 80-140,000 lire, $$$ = more than 140,000 lire.

Restaurants

ACQUA AL DUE
Via della Vigna Vecchia 40r
Tel: 284170
A good place to begin an acquaintance with Tuscan food, since this restaurant specialises in *assaggio*, a succession of little dishes which enables you to taste a great range of *antipasti*, followed by a series of different pastas and sauces. You can also sample a variety of desserts. Closed Monday; reservations advised. $

ANGIOLINO
Via Santo Spirito 36
Tel: 298976
The waiters are somewhat brusque (or at least pretend to be, to the delight of regulars) but the food is good, relatively cheap and authentic. Closed Sunday and Monday. $

ANTICO FATTORE
Via Lambertesca 1r
Tel: 238 1215
Food for both body and mind; pasta in ample proportions in this haunt of the literati; tripe cooked with tomatoes is also a speciality. Closed Sunday, Monday and August. $

BELLA CINA
Via Guelfa 24
Tel: 219201
This Chinese restaurant offers pleasant atmosphere, reasonable food, good service and usually a table or two filled with Chinese customers. $

IL BARONE DI PORTA ROMANA
Piazza Santo Spirito 6
Tel: 210437
Rustic-style trattoria/pizzeria with outdoor dining in the leafy square in summer. A wide selection of pizzas cooked authentically in a wood-fired oven. Closed Sunday and Monday lunch. $

RISTORANTE A BOLOGNESE
Borgo S. Lorenzo 31/r
Tel: 287481
Unusually stylish and inexpensive self-service place with pasta at 6,000 lire, chicken or beef 10,000 lire.

BUCA DELL'ORAFO
Volta dei Girolami 228r
Tel: 213619
Tiny but spirited cellar-restaurant by the Ponte Vecchio serving good-value *bistecca* and pasta. Closed Sunday lunch. $$

BUCA LAPI
Via del Trebbio 1r
Tel: 213768
In the cellar of the Palazzo Antinori; regarded as serving the best *bistecca alla Fiorentina* in town, plus an excellent range of local wines. Closed Sunday. $$

IL CAFFE
Piazza dei Pitti
Tel: 239 6241
Pavement café offering fixed price lunches opposite Pitti Palace. Espe-

The classic combination

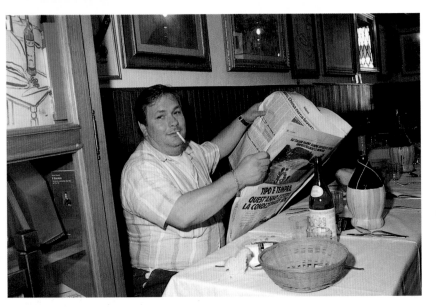

Well-fed at Il Latine – see page 76

cially pleasant on Mondays when the palace is closed and the cafe is thus less busy. Music some evenings. $$

CANTINETTA ANTINORI
Piazza Antinori 3
Tel: 292234
A showcase for the wines and other products of the Antinori family, one of Tuscany's oldest and most respected wine-makers. Offers light snacks of delicious *crostini* (appetisers on toasted bread) or full meals, complete withthe ambience of an 15th-century palazzo. Closed Saturday, Sunday, August and public holidays. Reservations are advised. $$

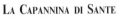

LA CAPANNINA DI SANTE
Piazza Ravenna
Tel: 688345
Specialises in fish, which is-absolutely fresh. Try the *spaghetti di mare* (with seafood) for a real feast. Closed Sunday, Monday lunch and August. $$

IL CAVALLINO
Via delle Farine 6r
Tel: 215818
Though the entrance is on a side street, there is an outdoor dining area in Piazza della Signoria, a romantic place to eat, with a view of the Palazzo Vecchio. Genuine Tuscan food and a good choice for Sundays, when many other restaurants are closed. Closed Tuesday evening. $$

CIBREO
Via dei Macci 118r
Tel: 234 1100
Simple décor and authentic Tuscan cuisine from cold tripe salad to boned leg of lamb stuffed with artichoke – but no pasta dishes. You pay lower prices for much the same menu if you go round the corner and eat in the *trattoria* section at the back, entered from Piazza Ghiberti 35r. Closed Sunday, Monday and August. $$

COCO LEZZONE
Via del Parioncino 26
Tel: 287178
Crowded and chaotic restaurant in which you can sample real Tuscan

74

peasant dishes such as *pappa al pomodoro* (bread, tomato and basil soup), *ribollita* (bread, beans and cabbage soup), Florentine-style tripe in tomato sauce and herb-flavoured roast pork. Closed Sunday, Tuesday evening and during August. $

DA NOI
Via Fiesolana 46r
Tel: 242917
Intimate restaurant serving creative variations on a Tuscan theme – the sort of dishes that foodies rave about. Dinner only, closed Sunday, Monday, August and Christmas; reservations essential. $$$

DE MEDICI
Via Giglio 57
Tel: 21878
A bright, elegant and slightly formal restaurant-piano bar that's worth the extravagance. $$

ENOTECA PINCHIORRI
Via Ghibellina 87
Tel: 242777
Another gourmet paradise, garlanded with awards and hailed by some as one of the best restaurants in Europe, scorned, by others, as pretentious, over-priced and over-rated. Make up your own mind if you are wealthy enough. Specialises in traditional Tuscan dishes. Also offers an outstanding wine-list and courtyard for summer dining. Closed Sunday, Monday lunch and August; reservations essential – best to book at least a week in advance. $$$

LE FONTICINE
Via Nazionale 78
Tel: 282106
This is a popular and atmospheric restaurant serving perfect pasta and juicy *bistecca*. Closed Monday and during August. $$

GANESH
Via del Giglio 26,
Tel: 289 634
The soft mellow lighting, the murals and the statue of the elephant all contribute to the elegance of this fine Indian restaurant. $$

TRATTORIA DA GIOVANNI
Via Guelfa 94r
An old-fashioned family place offering personal attention and very low prices. Rear garden. $

Service at Harry's Bar

HARRY'S BAR
Lungarno Vespucci 22r
Tel: 239 6700
An entertaining place modelled on the original Harry's Bar in Venice, made famous by Hemingway. The cocktail bartender is a real showman. The restaurant serves good beefburgers and American-influenced Italian food. Closed Sunday. $$

I CHE C'E C'E
Via Magalotti 11r
Tel: 216589
The name means 'What there is, there is', but this does not mean a lack of choice or a 'take it or leave it attitude'. The range of *crostini* (appetisers on toast), and the buffet of *antipasti* is superb and the daily specials are al-

ways unusual. The restaurant has many regulars and a friendly atmosphere. Closed Monday. $

IL LATINE
Via del Palchetti 6r
Tel: 210916
This is a sprawling noisy restaurant with communal tables. Expect to queue, but not for too long as the turnover is fast. The reward for this discomfort is good, filling Tuscan food

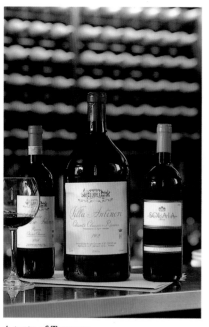

A taste of Tuscany

at very reasonable prices and more often than not the chance to make new friends. Closed Monday, Tuesday lunch, late July to early August and Christmas. $

OTELO
Via degli Orti Oricellari 36r
Tel: 215819
Just a few steps from the railway station and serving classical Tuscan cuisine and humbler dishes. Closed Tuesday. $$

PEKING
Via Melarancho 21
Tel: 282 922
Just across from Ganesh near the San Lorenzo market. Attractive decor and good food. $

SABATINI
Via Panzani 41
Tel: 211559
Sober setting for a restaurant that has gained an international reputation for polished service and traditional Tuscan dishes; try *pappardelle alla lepre* or *alla cinghiale* (homemade pasta with wild hare or wild boar sauce) and anything containing the magic words *funghi* (wild mushrooms) or *asparagi* (asparagus). Closed Monday in winter; reservations advised. $$$

SOSTANZA
Via del Porcellana 25r
Tel: 212691
Sostanza is a long-established *trattoria* (founded 1869), very plain and down-to-earth but patronised by many famous guests from Ezra Pound to Ronald Reagan. Equally famous is the speciality *petto di pollo al burro*, mouthwatering chicken breast in butter. Closed Saturday and Sunday. $$

Nightlife

Florence is basically a provincial town and its nightlife is relatively low-key and civilised. Florentines do not, on the whole, burn the night away in a frenetic trawl from one club or discotheque to another. Most Florentines prefer a leisurely meal and a stroll round their city in the cool of the night. Entertainment venues divide between piano bars for the older generation and, for the young, discos (barely tolerated by the local authority) and cafés. The nightly *passeggiata* between the two main piazzas is worth catching (*see page 62*).

The tourist authority (APT) puts out a monthly poster – the Calendario delle Manifestazione (Calendar of Events) – which is displayed in most hotels; this is not a comprehensive guide, but it does list all the major events and your hotel concierge may well be willing to phone and book tickets on your behalf (or you can apply to the central box-office at Via della Pergola 10; tel: 243361).

Alternatively, call at the tourist information office at Via Cavour 1r (next door to the Palazzo Medici-Riccardi); here there is a noticeboard displaying details of all the events of the day that can be enjoyed by English-speaking visitors, covering everything from films to jazz, rock and classical concerts, opera, dance and theatre. The staff will also help with bookings.

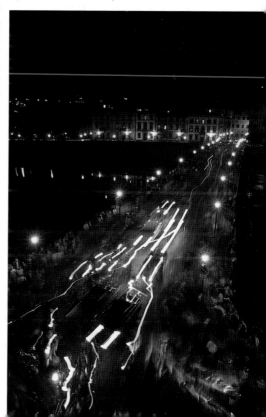

Night-time on the Arno at the Ponte alle Grazie

A drop to drink

Bars and Clubs

CAFE BE BOP
Via dei Servi 76r
Very young, jumpy place that doesn't come alive until 11pm. The admission charge includes one drink.

LA DOLCE VITA
Piazza del Carmine 6
Tel: 284595
Very fashionable late-night bar decorated in post-modernist style and hung with the work of local artists and photographers. Live music on Thursdays. Closed Sunday.

FIDDLER'S ELBOW
Piazza Santa Maria Novella 7r
Tel: 216056
Straight out of James Joyce's Dublin, an Irish bar with real character serving Guinness and other imported beers. Popular with English and Americans. Open 4pm–1am. Smoky.

GUIBBE ROSSE
Piazza della Repubblica 13r
Tel: 212280
Named after the red jackets of the waiters and historically a haunt of artists and intellectuals, it is now an expensive spot to enjoy drinks, snacks and ice-cream whilst watching the busy nightlife of the square.

JAZZ CLUB
Via Nuova dei Caccini 3
Tel: 247 9700
Live jazz and a good range of beers.

Pizza gossip

PASZKOWSKI
Piazza della Repubblica 6
Tel: 210236
Very grand piano bar (sometimes there is a small orchestra as well) playing light music and popular melodies; very popular with those old enough to remember when the songs were new. Closed Monday.

REX CAFE
Via Fiesalana 25r
Cafe Rex is a good, rambling bar popular with the younger artistic community in Florence.

RIFLISSI D'EPOCHA
Via de' Renai 13r
This is a popular and stylish basement club which specialises in jazz and blues music, with a video bar serving beer and cocktails. Open 9.30pm–6am. Entry free.

RIVOIRE
Piazza della Signoria 5r
Tel: 214412
This café provides the best views of the Palazzo Vecchio and is the perfect place to while away a romantic moonlit evening over wine; cocktails, ice-cream or delicious pastries. Closed Monday and the last two weeks in January.

Cinema

ASTRO
Piazza San Simone (Via Isola delle Stinche, near S. Croce)
This cinema shows English-language films every night of the week except Monday.

Discos

CAPITALE
Via del Fosso Macinante 2-4
Tel: 356723
Dancing out of doors. Relaxed atmosphere. From 10pm.

DOCTOR NO
Via dei Benci 19r
A must for young people, popular rock bands and live concerts.

ROCK CAFE
Borgo degli Albizi 66r
Tel: 244662
Live music plus disco. From 10pm.

SPACE ELECTRONIC
Via Palazzuolo 37
Tel: 293082
Ultra-modern disco with videos, lasers, light shows and a giant spaceship that wanders around the dance floor. From 9.30pm. Closed Monday.

TENAX
Via Pratese 47
Tel: 37050
Temax offers occasional live acts from international stars. The music is mainly rock and new wave. The leading club for arty, fashionable Florentines. From 10pm.

YAB YUM
Via dei Sasseti 5
Tel: 282018
Fashionable and central, set in a vast basement, but still crowded. From 11pm. Closed Monday, Wednesday, July and August.

Calendar of Special Events

JANUARY – APRIL

Music-lovers should check listings magazines to see what is on at the Teatro Pergola, Via della Pergola 12 (tel: 247 9651); during the first three months of the year the Amici della Musica (Friends of Music) organise a programme of chamber concerts.

Shrove Tuesday: a low-key event in Florence, but nearby villages celebrate with firewords and processions, most notably in Viareggio.

25 March: the normally quiet Piazza delle Santissima Annunziata comes alive to the sounds of excited children celebrating the feast of the Annunciation.

Easter: the **Scoppio del Carro** (Explosion of the Cart) takes place in the Piazza del Duomo and ostensibly celebrates the Resurrection, though pre-Christian fertility rites may actually underlie the custom. Crowds gather in the piazza to watch an 18th-century painted cart, in the shape of a tower, being drawn by white oxen to the cathedral doors. If proceedings go according to plan, a rocket in the shape of a dove then swoops from the high altar through the cathedral doors and ignites fireworks that are hidden in the carriage. The size and success of this conflagration serves as an omen indicating the likely outcome of that year's harvest.

MAY – JULY

Maggio Musicale (Musical May), the city's major arts festival, is no longer confined to May, nor to music; concerts, classical and contemporary dance performances and opera are all now included and the events last through May and June and into July.

Details of the festival can be obtained from Teatro Communale, Via Solferino 15, tel: 277 9236.

As Maggio Musicale tails out, the **Estate Fiesolana** (Fiesole Summer) arts festival picks up the baton with a celebration of music, drama and film from the end of June to the end of August. Most of the events take place in the Teatro Romana (Roman Theatre) in Fiesole, and at the Badia Fiesolana. Details from the tourist information office in Piazza Mino, Fiesole, tel: 598720.

First Sunday after Ascension Day: the **Festa del Grillo** (Cricket Festival) can be viewed as a religious festival or it can simply be seen as a celebration of the joys of spring. Cascine Park, to the west of the city centre, fills with stalls selling crickets which are then released to ensure good luck.

Calcio in Costume: literally translated, this means 'Football in Costume' (the teams wear 16th-century costumes) and it is played on June 19,

Fireworks in Piazzale Michelangelo

there is a big firework display over the city, beginning at 10pm. Get a place on the north bank of the Arno for the best view

Festa della Rificolona (Lantern Festival): this is a much more low-key, but enchanting, festival which takes place on September 7, the eve of the Birth of the Virgin. Children join in processions from all parts of the city, congregating in Piazza della Santissima Annunziata, carrying paper lanterns on sticks, containing lighted candles.

During October and December: look out again for chamber concerts at the Teatro Pergola organised by the Amici della Musica.

24 and 28, usually in Piazza Santa Croce (but check – sometimes it is held in Piazza della Signoria and sometimes in the Boboli Gardens).

The game is played by four teams, representing the four original *rioni*, or districts, of the city. It is a cross between football and rugby, but there are few observable rules. The rivalry is intense and tactics sometimes vicious.

Each match is accompanied by a magnificent costumed procession. The game held on June 24 is the most spectacular because it coincides with Midsummer and the Feast of St John the Baptist, the patron saint of Florence; celebrations last long into night and

Concerts are also given in winter by the Orchestra Regionale Toscana in the church of Santo Stefano al Ponte and by various other musical groups in many of the city's other churches. The main opera season is October to March, with performances at the Teatro Comunale, Corso Italia 16, and the Palazzo Vecchio.

Calcio in Costume, Piazza Santa Croce

PRACTICAL information

GETTING THERE

By Air

The cheapest way to get to Florence is to fly to Pisa's Galileo Galilei Airport and take the train. Plenty of airlines offer scheduled and charter flights to Pisa but advance reservations are essential in the summer. The airport is pleasantly informal, yet efficient, and offers exchange, car rental, shopping and duty-free facilities. For airport information, tel: (050) 28088.

Train tickets are bought at the kiosk to the left of the customs exit and Pisa Aeroporta railway station is located immediately to the left of the airport exit doors. Trains leave at least once every hour for Florence and the journey takes an hour.

Some airlines now fly direct to Florence Peretola airport 2 miles (4km) northwest of the city centre, though these flights tend to be more expensive than flights to Pisa. You can also fly to Peretola from Milan, Rome and Venice using Italy's domestic airline, ATI. Airport information, tel: 373498.

By Rail

The main railway station in Florence, Santa Maria Novella, is served by fast intercity and sleeper connections from all over Europe, including the Italia Express from Strasbourg and the Palatino service from Paris. Ask your local travel agent for details; reservations are essential and the cost (depending on the distance travelled) may be greater than a charter flight, unless you hold a rail pass that qualifies you for reduced fares. Information in Florence, tel: 278785.

Destination Florence

By Road

If you can bear the long, uncomfortable journey, there are plenty of coach services to Florence from European capitals. However, as is the case with travelling by train, you may find that flying is almost as cheap.

Travelling by car is not recommended if only because you will have problems once you arrive; traffic is banned from the historic centre and parking is very difficult (the only car-park of any size is in the Fortezza da Basso, northeast of the city centre, behind the railway station). If you do decide to drive to Florence, your best bet for a worry-free holiday is to find accommodation which offers its own secure parking.

Scooters are favoured by locals

When to Visit

Although Florence is an all-year-round destination, the heat and crowds of July and August are best avoided; likewise the crowds and queues can also be unbearable at Easter. If you are coming to Florence for just a few days, try to avoid Sunday afternoon and Monday when most of the city's museums, shops and restaurants are closed. May is probably the best month to see Florence, but June, September and October are also relatively cool and peaceful.

November to March can be wetter and colder than you would believe possible in a Mediterranean climate but, to compensate, the city will be far less crowded and you will probably find bargain price air fares and hotel rooms. If you want to visit Florence during the Calcio in Costume festival you would be wise to book at least six months in advance.

Visas and Passports

Nationals of the US, EU and Commonwealth countries need only an up-to-date passport to enter Italy. Other nationals should apply for a visa in advance from the nearest Italian consulate in their home country.

Vaccinations

None is required.

Customs

Items intended for your personal use can be imported duty-free and there are no limitations on the import of currency. EU residents aged 17 years or over can import the following duty-free (non-EU residents have the same limits, except that the tobacco allowance is doubled; higher limits apply to goods purchased within the EU):

Tobacco: 200 cigarettes or 100 cigarellos or 50 cigars or 250 grammes of tobacco.

Alcohol: 1 litre of spirits or 2 litres of still, sparkling or fortified wine.

Toiletries: 60 grammes of perfume or 250cc of toilet water.

Weather and Clothing

Winter in Florence can be bitingly cold but is often clear and sunny, so the city looks marvellous, although you will need an overcoat, gloves and hat to enjoy it. Winter can last until Easter and the short spring is often marked by heavy rain. Thereafter temperatures rise rapidly to 25°C (78°F) or more for the months of May to September. Florentines judge people very much on the basis of personal appearance so dress well, in smart casual clothes, rather than slumming it in untidy shorts, T-shirts and trainers. September to November are the wettest months, when a raincoat is indispensable.

What to Bring

Binoculars are useful if you want to study frescos in detail, since many of them are located high up on church walls.

Electricity

The supply is 220 volts and the plugs are standard mainland Europe type, with two round pins. You will need an adaptor to use British three-pin appliances and a transformer if the appliances normally operate at 100-120 volts (eg, US and Canadian standard).

Time

Italy observes Central European Time (one hour ahead of Greenwich Mean Time) from October to April. Italian clocks then go forward by an hour.

Currency

The Italian *lira* (plural *lire*) is usually abbreviated to L or £. The lira is now a relatively stable currency, but this has not been true in the past when inflation was rampant – hence you must get used to prices in the hundreds of thousands of lire (1 million lire is worth around £450 or US$760, less than the average visitor's budget for a week). Many Italians would like the government to simplify the currency by knocking off three noughts (ie, 1,000 lire would become 1 lira), but so far this measure has been defeated every time it comes to a parliamentary vote.

Notes come in denominations of 1,000, 2,000, 5,000, 10,000, 50,000 and 100,000 lire; coins in denominations of 50, 100, 200 and 500 lire. Telephone tokens (*gettoni*) are also accepted as coinage: their current value is 200 lire. Coins and small notes are no longer in short supply, and you should not have difficulty getting change for a 50,000-lire note – but it is worth keeping a supply of 1,000-lire notes for small purchases, such as a cup of coffee, a postcard or museum admission fees. You will also need a supply of 100- and 200-lire coins to feed into the electricity meters in churches so that you can illuminate the frescos.

Credit Cards

The major credit cards (Visa, Mastercard/Access, American Express and Diners Club) are accepted in many hotels, restaurants and upmarket shops (look for a sign saying *Carta Si* – 'Card Yes' – in the window).

Cash Machines

You can obtain lire from cash machines displaying a blue and red EC sign if your credit card displays the same symbol. You will need to key in the correct PIN number (check with your bank or card company before you go if you have forgotten your PIN number). The system is not infallible and if the machine swallows your card, you can usually retrieve it by presenting your passport to the bank within three days. This is an expensive way of gaining money, since you pay a handling charge of around 1.5 per cent and interest is charged at a very high rate from the moment you obtain the cash; it could, however, be useful in an emergency.

Several banks in Florence also have automatic exchange machines into which you can feed bank notes (those of the major European currencies or US dollars) and receive lire in return. Instructions are given in several languages and the exchange rate is the same as that offered by banks; the machines are, though, apt to reject notes that are creased or damaged.

Exchange

Eurocheques are widely accepted and are as good as money: each cheque can be cashed at a bank for up to 30,000 lire. Traveller's cheques are also easy to exchange, but remember to present your passport.

Banks offer the best rates and are normally open Monday to Friday from 8.20am to 1.20pm. Some banks also open in the afternoon from 2.30pm to 3.45pm. The Banco Nazionale at the railway station is open continuously from 8.20am to 7.20pm Monday to Saturday. Outside these hours and at weekends you can always use automatic exchange machines. Small exchange booths often charge up to three percent commission.

Farmacias can help with minor ailments

prescription in other countries. Normal opening hours are 9am–1pm and 4pm–7pm Monday to Friday. The address of the nearest *farmacia* on emergency duty will be posted in the window. The Farmacia Comunale, at the railway station, is open all night.

Medical Services

Call the Tourist Medical Service, tel: 475411, for advice. The service is available 24 hours and a doctor will visit you in your hotel if necessary. In an emergency, tel: 212222 for an ambulance. The number for the heart attack first aid unit is 214444. Every public hospital in Florence has a casualty department (Pronto Soccorso) where treatment is free. The most central in Florence is the Ospedale Santa Maria Nuova, Piazza Santa Maria Nuova, tel: 27581. Otherwise, medical care has to be paid for. EU nationals should obtain form E111 from post offices or health and social security departments in advance of their visit and follow the instructions to obtain a reimbursement of the costs. Others should take out travel insurance providing cover for emergency medical care.

Tipping

Tips are not expected, but they are appreciated. Service charge is included in most restaurant bills but you may wish to leave a little extra for good service. 1,000 lire is an adequate tip for taxi drivers and porters.

USEFUL INFORMATION

Geography and Economy

Florence is the capital of Tuscany and lies on the Arno river, 50 miles/80km inland from the sea. The Arno valley and the plain to the west of Florence are heavily built up and industrialised; glass-making, motorcycle manufacture, textiles and gold-working are among the major industries, as well as intensive horticulture and market-gardening.

Florence itself (pop: 500,000) is a major centre for artisan-based industries, for example, *haute couture*, textile manufacture, leather-working and paper-making; in addition, it has a thriving service sector, which includes banking, legal services and insurance.

HEALTH AND EMERGENCIES

Pharmacies

A *farmacia* is identified by a cross, often red and usually neon at night. The shops are staffed by trained pharmacists who can prescribe drugs, including antibiotics, that are only available by doctor's

Crime

Florence is a relatively safe city but you still need to take sensible precautions to avoid pickpocketing or theft. Keep photocopies of important documents separately from the originals, to help the replacement process if they are lost or stolen. If you need to report a theft, go to the police station (*questura*) on Via Zara 2 (tel: 49771) and make a statement (*denuncia*) using an official multilingual form, keeping one stamped copy for yourself as evidence for making an insurance claim.

The *Vigili Urbana* are traffic police whose main job is to prevent infringement of parking regulations and keep unauthorised vehicles out of the centre during prohibited hours. Local police matters are handled by the *Polizia Urbana*. If you need them in an emergency, dial 113. You may also see armed police – the *Carabinieri*; they are a national police force, technically a branch of the army, which deals with serious crime.

Toilets

Some museums have public toilets but elsewhere they scarcely exist. Toilets in bars are for customer use, so buy a coffee first and ask for the *bagno, toilette* or *gabinetto*. One toilet may serve for both sexes; otherwise they may be marked *signore* or *donne* for women and *signori* or *uomini* for men.

GETTING AROUND

Florence is so compact that you really can walk everywhere. You may, however, want to take the occasional taxi if you are carrying luggage or are out late at night. You will find taxi ranks at the railway station and in most main streets and piazzas. For a radio taxi, tel: 4390 or 4798.

Buses

Buses in Florence are bright orange in colour and are run by ATAF. To save time trying to work out all the routes, simply remember that most buses pass through, and can be caught from, Piazza del Duomo or Santa Maria Novella station. Bus numbers and routes are clearly displayed at each bus-stop.

Tickets are not available on the bus and must be bought in advance from bars and tobacco shops displaying the ATAF sticker. You will also find ticket-dispensing machines in the street alongside main bus-stops. The ticket should be fed into the stamping machine at the rear of the bus on entry. Each ticket is valid for 60 minutes' travel, during which time you can change from one bus to another as often as you need.

Maps and Guides

The most detailed map of Florence is published by LAC (Litografia Artistica Cartografica) and is called *Firenze: Pianta della Citta*. Of guides currently available, *Insight Guide: Florence* (Apa Publications) is the best for getting beneath the skin of the Florentines, whilst the Agostini guide to *Florence* (Istituto Geografico de Agostini, 1987) is the best fcomprehensive guide to monuments. Most museums in Florence now also sell

Taxis by the Duomo

excellent illustrated guides to their own collections. The travel bookshop called Libreria Viaggio, Borgo degli Albizi r41 (tel: 240 489)r, stocks a very good range of maps and guides to Florence and the rest of the world. A good English bookshop is Paperback Exchange, Via Fiesolana r31.

Tourist Offices

The main office is at Via Manzoni 16 (tel: 247 8141) but this is a long way out of the city centre and is only open to the public in the mornings (9am–1pm, closed Sunday). Much more useful are the two branch offices in the centre. One is located in an alley south of Piazza della Signoria (Chiasso Baroncelli 17) while the other is next to the Medici-Riccardi Palace (Via Cavour 1r). Both are open to personal callers only (no telephone service) and are usually open daily 9am–7pm. Remember, too, that your hotel concierge will probably prove as knowledgeable and helpful as tourist office staff.

ACCOMMODATION

Hotels

Hotels in Florence are graded and priced according to their facilities. Cheap accommodation (1- or 2-star) does exist, especially along Via Nazionale from the railway station, but most hotels in Flo-

rence are in the 3-star category or above
– quite expensive, in other words. However, you often get to stay in historic
buildings of considerable grandeur. It is
best to book ahead, especially for Christmas, Easter and summer holiday periods.
There is a room-booking agency at the
railway station, open 9am–8.30pm, whose
services are available to personal callers.

Price categories (for a double room): $
= up to $50, $$ = up to $80 and $$$ =
around or over $100.

ALBA
Via della Scala 22
Tel: 282610
Comfort at reasonable prices. **$$–$$$**

ANNELANA
Via Romana 34
Tel: 222402/3
Antique-furnished rooms in a 15th-century former convent, built as a refuge for
the widows of the nobility. **$$–$$$**

APRILE
Via della Scala 6
Tel: 216237
Appealing hotel with a range of rooms
to suit most pockets. **$$**

PENSIONE BERNA
Largo Alinari 11
Tel: 287701
Near the station. Ten clean, inexpensive
rooms. **$**

BERNINI PALACE
Piazza San Firenze 29
Tel: 288621
Upmarket, with frescoed dining-room
and views of the Palazzo Vecchio. **$$$**

BRUNELLESCHI
Piazza Santa Elisabeta 3
Tel: 562068
Located in a tiny central piazza and
partly housed in a church with a 6th-century tower. Luxurious. **$$$**

CALZAIUOLI
Via del Calzaiuoli 6
Tel: 212456
In a 19th-century palazzo. Central. **$$$**

CAVOUR
Via del Proconsolo 3
Tel: 282461
Recently modernised luxury hotel in the
14th-century Palazzo Strozzi-Ridolfi.
Ffine views from the roof-garden. **$$–$$$**

CROCE DI MALTA
Via della Scala 7
Tel: 218351
Intimate hotel in a former convent with
pool, garden and fine restaurant. **$$$**

LE DUE FONTANE
Piazza Santissima Annunziata 14
Tel: 280086
Small modern hotel located on a quiet
square. Parking. **$$–$$$**

EXCELSIOR
Piazza Ognissanti 3
Tel: 264201
Old-world grandeur combined with all
modern conveniences; polished service,
luxurious rooms and fine Arno views
from the roof-garden. Private parking.
Very expensive. **$$$**

FERRETTI
Via delle Belle Donne 17
Tel: 238 1328
Cheap but clean and comfortable *pensione* near the station. Favoured by impoverished art students and writers and
run by friendly Anglophile owners. **$**

Local flavour

HOTEL GLOBUS
Via San Antonia 24
Tel: 211062
Globus offers inexpensive elegance only a few paces away from the San Lorenzo Market. $

HELVETIA & BRISTOL
Via dei Pescioni 2
Tel: 287814
Very central grand hotel, newly refurbished and full of antiques. Parking. Very expensive. $$$

JENNINGS RICCIOLI
Corso Tintori 7
Tel: 244751/2
This hotel is famous as the setting for E. M. Forster's *A Room with a View* (Room 21, with its distant view of San Miniato al Monte). Recently restored. Private parking. $

HERMITAGE
Vicolo Marzio 1, Piazza del Pesce
Tel: 287216
Very central hotel offerin good views of the Ponte Vecchio, although you may prefer the quieter, viewless rooms at the back. $$–$$$

LOGGIATA DEI SERVITI
Piazza Santissima Annunziata 3
Tel: 289592
Arguably the most characterful small hotel in Florence; set in a 16th-century convent on the quiet piazza opposite Innocenti, every room furnished with antiques. Good value. $$$

LUNGARNO
Borgo San Jacopo 14
Tel: 264211
Modern hotel, very popular for its views of the Ponte Vecchio from the front rooms. Private parking. $$$

MINERVA
Piazza Santa Maria Novella 16
Tel: 284555
This is an elegant, expensive hotel offering lovely views from the rooftop swimming pool and a garden restaurant. Private parking. $$$

MONNA LISA
Borgo Pinti 27
Tel: 247 9751
Characterful hotel occupying a 14th-century palazzo, furnished with paintings and antiques. The quieter rooms, overlooking the courtyard garden, are the best. $$$

PITTI PALACE
Via Barbadori 2
Tel: 239 8711
A small, traditional hotel just south of the Ponte Vecchio, popular with English-speaking visitors because the co-owner is American. Private parking. $$–$$$

QUISISANA E PONTEVECCHIO
Lungarno Archibusieri 4
Tel: 216692
The location for James Ivory's film of Forster's *A Room with a View*. $$–$$$

SAVOY
Piazza della Repubblica 7
Tel: 283313
The Savoy offers grand, if somewhat faded, *fin-de-siècle* luxury in the heart of the city. $–$$

HOTEL UNIVERSO
Piazza Santa Maria Novella
Tel: 281951
Sleek, modern hotel sharing piazza with the Grand Hotel Minerva but at half the price. $$$

Hotel Villa Aurora
Piazza Mino 39,
Fiesole
Tel: 59100
Luxurious palace elegantly furnished and-set in hills overlooking Florence. Good terrace restaurant and bar. $$–$$$

Villa San Michele
Via Doccia 4,
Fiesole
Tel: 59451
The most luxurious of the city's grand luxe hotels, located in a former Franciscan monastery in Fiesole. Partly designed by Michelangelo. $$$

Wanda
Via Ghibelline 51
Tel: 234 484
Run by a friendly lady of the same name in a former palace, two rooms are adorned with frescoes. $$

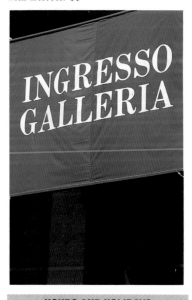

Business Hours

Shops generally open during the week Tuesday to Saturday 9am–1pm and from 4–7pm. Many are closed all day Monday or at least for the morning. Flower and cake shops open in the morning on Sundays and public holidays, when Floren-tines like to treat themselves and each other, but little else operates thens, although bars remain open all day, every day. Many businesses, including restaurants, close for two weeks in August, the traditional holiday month in Italy.

Museums and Monuments

Specific information on opening hours is given in the itinerary section of this book, but the opening hours are notoriously subject to change at short notice. Many hotels keep a list of the latest opening times for their guests to consult, so check before you set out and remember that most museums are closed on Monday.

Churches are usually open 7am–noon and from 4–7pm (or dusk in winter).

Public Holidays

Most businesses are closed on the following national holidays:
January 1
January 6 (Epiphany)
Good Friday
Easter Monday
April 25 (Liberation Day)
May 1 (Labour Day)
August 15 (Assumption)
November 1 (All Saints)
December 8 (Immaculate Conception)
December 25 and 26

In addition to these public holidays, many businesses close for the period June 23–28 when the city celebrates the feast of its patron saint, St John the Baptist. August is the official holiday month in Italy when some shops and restaurants will be closed.

You will have no difficulty in buying the major European newspapers, although you may find they are a day late. If you read Italian, the daily *La Nazione* and *La Repubblica* contain details of local entertainment and events. Cultural events are listed in two English-language listings magazine, often available in hotels or from tourist information centres, called *Florence Today* and *Florence Concierge Information*.

POST AND TELECOMMUNICATIONS

Tobacconists sell postage stamps for letters and postcards: look for a sign with the white letter T on a blue background. For other transactions go to the central post office (Palazzo delle Poste) at Via Pelliceria 160, near Piazza della Repubblica, open Monday to Friday, 8.15am–7pm and Saturday until noon.

Coin-operated phones accept 100-, 200- and 500-lire coins and can be found in many streets and squares; you can also phone from a bar if it displays the sign of a red telephone handset in a red circle. Insert the coins before you dial and insert more if you hear a beep while you are still speaking; unused coins will be refunded after your call by pushing the return button. Many public phones also accept phone cards (*carta telefonica*), costing 5,000 or 10,000 lire, which can be bought in many tobacconists.

Telephone booths for long-distance or overseas calls are located in the central post office (open 24 hours, Via Pelliceria 160) and the railway station (open 8am to 9.45pm Monday to Saturday). Here you can make metered calls and pay by cash or credit card. To get an international line, dial 00.

To dial a local number, omit the area code; otherwise you need to dial the city or district code, then the subscriber number. The engaged tone consists of a series of rapid pips; the dialling tone is a series of longer notes. When Italians answer the phone they invariably say *pronto* (meaning 'ready').

The area code for Florence is 055; confusingly, telephone numbers in the city can have 4, 5, 6 or 7 digits.

FACILITIES FOR THE DISABLED

Nearly all the museums in Florence have wheelchair ramps and lifts. A useful publication *Access to Florence*, can be obtained from Mrs V Saunders, Project Phoenix Trust, 68 Rochfords, Coffee Hall, Milton Keynes, MK6 5DJ

FURTHER READING

Of the many good books written about Florence, Mary McCarthy's *The Stones of Florence and Venice Observed* (Penguin) is the most stimulating, but it assumes that you already possess a considerable knowledge of the city. As basic primers, try J R Hale's *Florence and the Medici* (Thames and Hudson), Irving Stone's *The Agony and the Ecstasy*; Penguin's *The Portable Renaissance Reader,* or Christopher Hibbert's *The Rise and Fall of the House of Medici* (Penguin).

Airlines

AIR FRANCE
Borgo SS Apostoli 9
Tel: 055-218335

ALITALIA
Lungarno Acciaioli 10-12r
Tel: 055-27888

BRITISH AIRWAYS
Via Vigna Nuova 36r
Tel: 055-218655

IBERIA
Piazza Antinori 2
Tel: 055-215227

KLM ROYAL DUTCH AIRWAYS
Piazza Antinori 2
Tel: 055-284043

LUFTHANSA
Piazza Antinori 2
Tel: 055-2381444

OLYMPIC AIRWAYS
Via Por Santa Maria 4
Tel: 055-282338

SAS SCANDINAVIAN AIRLINES
Lungarno Acciaioli 8
Tel: 055-2382701

SWISSAIR
Via Parione 1
Tel: 055-295055/6

TWA
Piazza Santa Trinita 1r
Tel: 055-2382795

Sights that are open when everything else is closed

Sight	Open Sunday	Open Monday		Open over	Closing	Itinerary
	pm	am	pm	lunch	day	number
Duomo (cathedral)	Yes	Yes	Yes	Yes	None	Day 1
Cathedral dome	No	Yes	Yes	Yes	Sunday	Day 1
Giotto's campanile	Yes	Yes	Yes	Yes	None	Day 1
Palazzo Vecchio	No	Yes	Yes	Yes	Saturday	Day 1
Uffizi	No	No	No	Yes	Monday	Day 1
Boboli Gardens	Yes	No	No	Yes	Monday	Day 3
Forte Belvedere	Yes	Yes	Yes	Yes	None	Day 3
Brancacci Chapel	Yes	Yes	Yes	(except Sun)	Tuesday	Day 3
Santa Croce	Yes	Yes	Yes	No	None	Option 1
Innocenti	No	Yes	No	No	Wednesday	Option 2
Firenze com'era museum	No	Yes	No	No	Thursday	Option 2
Museo dell'Opera	No	Yes	Yes	Yes	Sunday	Option 3
Fiesole sights	Yes	Yes	Yes	Yes	None	Option 6
Medici villas	Yes	No	No	Yes	Monday	Option 7
Most churches	Yes	Yes	Yes	No	None	

Index

ACKNOWLEDGMENTS

Photography **Robert Mort** *and*
8/9 **Albano Guatti**
84 **G Galvin & G Taylor**

Handwriting **V Barl**
Cover Design **Klaus Geisler**
Production Editor **Mohammed Dar**
Cartography **Berndtson & Berndtson**